WHAT PEOPLE ARE SAYING ABOUT THE MILLIONAIRE'S MAP:

The Millionaires MAP is the most powerful prosperity tool I've yet to encounter in 20 years of studying money and personal development. It opened my eyes to my best financial future, and it opened my heart to my highest, greatest, grandest values because it also acts as an extraordinary clarifier of your passions. And I must add this: For the first time in my life I feel completely open and ready to receive millions, and I've never had so much fun with money as I did while working through the book's easy daily exercises. I highly recommend *The Millionaires MAP* to all my friends, because it works profoundly on so many levels. Thank you Matthew!

Patrick Combs, Bestselling author, Major In Success and Man 1, Bank 0;
inspirational speaker, entertainer, storyteller; Co-Founder, MIGHT

Please accept the following sincere and heartfelt words of thanks for *The Millionaire's MAP*. Seven years ago, my wife Mary and I moved our training company, and for various reasons and unfortunate circumstances, income from our thirty-year old business declined dramatically. A few months ago, our good friend Dr. Lou Savary kindly shared a copy of your book with us—and we proceeded to devour it with a passion. *The results have been extraordinary.* No sooner did we finish the book's exercises for a first time, new contracts began pouring in. We continue to experience even more dramatic results each time we repeat the exercises. There is no way Mary and I can thank you enough for *The Millionaire's MAP!*

Peter J. Esseff, Ph.D., Vice President & Technical Director, ESF Inc.
www.ESF-ProTrainer.com

The Millionaire's Map is **an extraordinary application of the natural laws of the universe which govern growth and increase**. In this book, Matthew Cross has created a wonderful process which offers the reader the opportunity to build a brighter future of prosperity, goodness and great well being for ourselves and our world.

Joan Andrews, President, Foundation for the American Indian and a former Director,
The Educational Foundation of America

Sometimes I feel the need to share something that has impacted my life for the better. *The Millionaires MAP has been a profound experience that keeps on unfolding in more and more wonderful ways.* Along with other personal processes, this book has helped me to see there are truly no limits to prosperity. It is not about how much money you have in the bank, it is a deep knowing that the universe is vast and unlimited. This book can be used again and again by anyone in any situation… and it works. Even if you do not believe in such things.

This is not just a book to read, but to do. It is fun and inspiring. I recommend you get this book for anyone you truly care about and would like to see living a more prosperous life.

GM Khalsa, Master Yogi & author, "Total Fitness"; www.BreathIsLife.com

The Millionaires MAP is *a ground breaking 21-day journey to the abundance that is rightfully ours*, if we simply ask for it.

By simply writing down how we want to spend the allotted amounts each day, we affirm that we not only deserve but we can have that which we yearn for. The first time I did it, it was at times difficult to decide how to spend and give to myself. Page by page, as I accumulated and spent my daily cash allotments, I became more and more comfortable. Soon it became as easy and effortless to make and spend money as it did during the exercises. All of this began to manifest in my life as abundance in ways I never imagined. The exercises in *The Millionaires MAP* make it easy and fun to transition from positive affirmations to an abundant reality.

Bruce Mandelbaum, Lic. Ac., LMT
Acupuncturist and Peak Performance Massage Therapist

The Millionaire's MAP offers you a key to access your inner powers of imagination and creation. Practicing spending money in this magic book gets our subconscious and conscious mind used to wealth and expansion. *It reconnects us to our higher purpose and helps us to make the invisible dreams and talents in our lives visible.* I recommend doing *The Millionaire's MAP* several times a year; I enjoy the process enormously and continue to experience wonderful results in my life.

Peter Donovan, Entrepreneur

After completing my first exercise of *The Millionaire's MAP*, I became my own president and started my consulting firm. ***I have a new determination for turning my desired outcomes into reality***. Reading this book and participating in this exercise helped me to discover the means to creating abundance in all areas of my life.

Ingrid Degand, Entrepreneur

This book has been instrumental in changing my life. Briefly, since I began working with *The Millionaire's MAP* my income has increased threefold. Initially, I was doing contract work which was filled with great opportunity, however, it was inconsistent. Working with *The Millionaire's MAP* I got steady work in the bottom of the Grand Canyon and so doubled my income! Recognizing the great potential I continued practicing the exercises in *The Millionaire's MAP*. Before the year was out I was offered a national position which more than doubled my income! I continue to observe that the principles taught in the *The Millionaire's MAP* work in my life. Because it is a process and a daily practice, it continues to infuse my life with POSSIBILITY. ***In the current economic climate I have gleaned the tools I need to create my next steps. It is genius. Thank you from the bottom of my heart!!!***

Dianne Duncan Perrote

THE MILLIONAIRE'$

MAP™

Chart Your Way to Wealth & Abundance
by Tapping the Infinite Power of Your Imagination

A 21-day interactive handbook based on the fascinating
Fibonacci Sequence 0, 1, 1, 2, 3, 5, 8, 13, 21...

You can have, do or be anything you want.
Abraham, www.abraham-hicks.com

Whatever you can do or dream you can, begin it.
Boldness has genius, power and magic in it. Begin it now.

Johann Wolfgang von Goethe

THE MILLIONAIRE'S MAP™

For more information contact:

Hoshin Media Company
P.O. Box 16791
Stamford, Connecticut 06905 USA

www.HoshinMedia.com

CONTENTS

0, 1, 1, 2, 3, 5, 8, 13, 21, 34, 55, 89, 144, 233, 377, 610, 987, 1597, 2584, 4181, 6765, 10946... The ratio *between* the numbers in the Fibonacci Sequence forever approaches 1.6180339... , the Golden Ratio/Proportion or Divine Code...

Look under your feet. The great opportunity is where you are.
Every place is under the stars; every place is the center of the universe.

John Burroughs

THE GOLDEN KEY$ TO WEALTH AND ABUNDANCE

On each day of the simple process which follows, you'll practice spending and enjoying increasing amounts of money—in the workshop of your imagination. The formula of increase that will guide your daily spending is known as the Fibonacci Sequence. This special, infinite sequence contains Nature's Golden Growth Code. This secret code has had many names throughout history. Simply put, it guides the growth, harmony and success of most everything in the universe. You'll learn more about this "Golden Key" to wealth and abundance in the following pages.

Another powerful yet underutilized key to wealth and abundance is this: *your subconscious mind doesn't know the difference between what is "real" and what is "imagined."* Imagination and reality are two sides of the same golden coin. The Millionaire's MAP will be your personal guide to a grand adventure in unlimited, wealthy imagination. Within these pages you'll automatically develop and strengthen a greater abundance mindset—the foundation for an abundant life. The process can also be enjoyed by couples—even families—who want to design a more abundant future together. The Millionaire's MAP holds the power to help you blueprint and prepare for a wealthier life, on all levels. If you want to be wealthy in your life the theory goes, you must first be wealthy in your heart and mind. The great news is, you can just as powerfully practice living in abundance working with imaginary money as you can with real money. And that's where this book comes in.

As you complete your easy daily Millionaire's MAP exercises, you may discover that the more reflective you are in considering how to spend your daily money allotment, the more you align with your guiding values and life purpose. One theory behind this is that what you want to do with your money reflects, at one level, what you want to do with your life. This concept is powerful because money is such a strong metaphor for the things we need, desire and value. When we look at money we actually see beyond it: we see what we think it can do for us, or what it can bring us— for example, security, freedom, love, friendship, approval, power. It's not money in and of itself we want. *It's what money represents.* Money is just the medium, a bridge to our deeper desires.

Money is also of course a universal symbol of value, regardless of which country's name is on the currency. For much of history, money has been represented by materials having intrinsic or real value, such as gold or silver. Nowadays, most money is represented by symbols and a promise. For example, the paper and ink used to create a dollar bill are worth little by themselves. Yet that same paper with special symbols printed on it—transformed into currency—represents value. Most often today, your money is represented by other symbols such as numbers on a ledger, or as digital symbols that show up only as electronic blips on your bank's computer screen. Money, in any of these symbolic forms, is simply what you exchange in order to get what you need and desire. So, whether you spend money in your hands or in your mind, you are really just working with symbols and energy. When you get right down to it, *money is simply energy made visible.* This includes gold or silver (and all matter), which quantum physics tells us is nothing more than atoms vibrating at a specific frequency. There is actually more "space" than matter in even the densest matter, with a matrix of vibrating energy blueprinting and holding it all in place.

In The Millionaire's MAP, you spend money—in increasing amounts—on paper. This journaling method is easy, fun and trackable. Yet again, it's not so much the money that's important—it's the *virtual* practice of spending increasing amounts of money, aligned with Nature's Golden Growth Code, that works the magic. Most people don't often practice unlimited imagination around wealth in their daily lives. The secret power of The Millionaire's MAP is that it lifts your perspective of abundance to a higher level and helps you keep it there. Simply playing the game opens the door to a more abundant and fulfilling future. And as Oliver Wendell Holmes observed: "A mind stretched to a new idea never goes back to its original dimensions."

The world is but a canvas to our imagination.
Henry David Thoreau

CORNUCOPIA:
LEGEND OF THE HORN OF PLENTY

The Cornucopia or "Horn of Plenty" is perhaps the oldest archetypal symbol of abundance. Said to have the power to give the person in possession of it whatever he or she wishes for, the word's origin says it all: An abundance or plentiful supply [*<Latin, cornu, horn + copia, plenty.*] A quick visit to the world of mythology adds fascinating richness to the story:

According to Greek mythology, when the young Zeus (Jupiter) was playing with Amalthea, the goat who had suckled him in a cave on the island of Crete, and gave him everything else he needed to survive, he accidentally broke off one of her horns. To make amends, Zeus promised that from that day forward, the horn would always be filled with whatever fruit she desired. As such, the Cornucopia came to symbolize the profusion of gifts from the gods. It has been used as an emblem of many deities, including Copia (Roman goddess of wealth and plenty who carries a Cornucopia), Justitia (Roman goddess of justice), Spes (Roman goddess of hope), Honos (Roman deity of morality and military honor), and many others. The myth of the horn returns in the story of Hercules, who fights the river-god Achelous, who, having the power to change himself into anything, took the form of a bull. Achelous was the son of the ocean, and the god of the biggest river. Hercules breaks off one of the bull's horns, but after generously returning it, receives from Achelous the horn of plenty—the Cornucopia. In Masonry, the Cornucopia symbolizes peace, plenty and joy. *(from the excellent Masonic knowledge site: www3.tky.3web.ne.jp/~jafarr/index.htm)*

As it turns out, the Cornucopia is borne directly of the Golden Growth Spiral, which also reflects the infinitely expanding Fibonacci Sequence. This is clearly seen in its origins as a Golden Spiral-shaped goat's horn, which naturally reflects the universal principle of harmonious growth and expansion. In the

Cornucopia's case, the increase in its size from a tiny Golden Spiral to a large open-ended horn only amplifies its Golden origins. Viewed in 3-D, it beautifully mirrors an expanding Nautilus shell. Cornucopia's were used on some of the earliest coins minted and could still be found all the way into the 1900's on some US currency and European coins. Cornucopia's are now mostly associated with harvest time and Thanksgiving, with no memory of their ancient Golden Growth Spiral origins. Interestingly, according to wikipedia.org, a "Cornucopian" is one who "holds any of a variety of views that are not in the ordinary sense simply optimistic about progress and confident in technological innovation, but see a limitlessly abundant future for humanity."

So, how would it feel to have access anytime to your own personal Horn of Plenty? Well, you're holding the key to it in your hands right now. The Millionaire's MAP perfectly reflects the spirit of the Cornucopia through its exponentially increasing Fibonacci Sequence daily spending pattern. While The Millionaire's MAP is lifting and magnetizing your attitude around abundance, it's also throwing the switch on your Cornucopia into the "on" position. Get ready to enjoy a bountiful harvest!

Given the right circumstances, from no more than dreams, determination, and the liberty to try, quite ordinary people do extraordinary things.
Dee Hock, Founder & CEO Emeritus, VISA International

Cornucopia on gate of Bank of America building in downtown Stamford, Connecticut.

Wealth, like a tree, grows from a tiny seed.
Wealth grows in magic ways.

George Clason, The Richest
Man in Babylon

HOW TO USE THIS BOOK

I like short and clear instructions, so here we go:

The aim of this book is to powerfully increase the wealth, abundance and quality of your life. If you're ready to upgrade the quality of your life and finances right now, then you ought to start right now. All you'll need is this handbook and a good pen or pencil. Here's how The Millionaire's MAP formula works:

❖ There are 21 chapters ahead, not including the 3 optional "Break Day" chapters. Each chapter is 4 pages long (feel free to skip the daily story and go right to filling in your daily spending record). You complete only 1 chapter a day—no more. Each chapter will likely take from 3 to 13 minutes to complete. The entire process takes 21 days. That's how long it takes to ignite your wealth transformation.

❖ Your assignment each day is the same, with a twist: You get to spend money on anything you like—in your imagination. On the right-hand pages you'll jot down your spending choices in your Daily Spending Record, as in the example on the opposite page (note that you can group multiple items into one spending amount, as in the Apple Store example). *The only thing that changes each day after Day 2 is the amount of money you get to spend.* Your daily spending amount increases according to the Fibonacci Sequence, which reflects Nature's Golden Growth Code. You'll learn more about this fascinating principle of exponential increase as you progress through the chapters. For now, know that each day after Day 2 promises a delightful increase in your daily spending money.

❖ During the 24 hours or so between chapters, your mind will be working diligently behind the scenes to prepare for the next chapter. These in-between hours are important for the success of The Millionaire's MAP process, as this is where your mind will learn to think, plan and act like a millionaire. Morning is a great time to do the process, as our mind is often clearer at the start of our day vs. at the end. When doing The Millionaire's MAP with another person, it's best to fill in each day together. The shared experience around your spending choices offers valuable opportunities for mutual growth. Now, turn the page and let's begin.

❖ Lastly, it's a good idea to use a colored pen (blue, red, green, purple, etc.) to fill in your daily spending record. *Color* activates creativity, learning and memory.

P.S. – The "MAP" in Millionaire's MAP is there because this process is both a "MAP" and a *Master Action Process* to enhance the wealth, abundance and quality of your life.

We could say the universe is made of possibilities, not atoms.
Muriel Rukeyser

Today's Date

8 / 13 / 09
_____

SPENDING RECORD

7

DAY SEVEN

Your total funds to
spend in full today is
$1,300

Today you receive $1,300 to spend. Jot down your items and their amounts.

No.	Items	Amount
1	Sent Mom Flowers	45.00
2	Apple Store (iPod, Portable Speakers, iPhone)	860.00
3	Lunch with Diana at Santa Cafe	55.00
4	4 copies of The Millionaires MAP for gifts	100.00
5	Pay off credit card balance	240.00
Total		**$1,300**

EXAMPLE

Insights from today's spending (optional):

_____ Really enjoyed my Apple Store spending spree... _____

was also fun deciding which flowers to send Mom. Next time I'll treat

_____ Diana to lunch at Teany Cafe. I can get used to this! _____

11

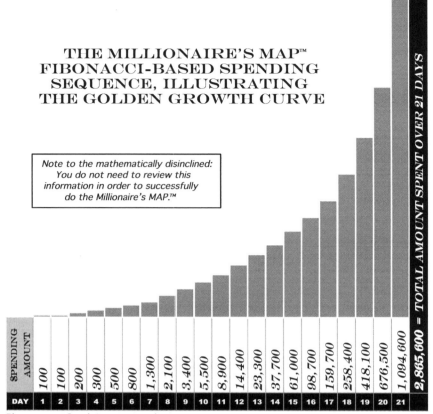

THE MILLIONAIRE'S MAP™ FIBONACCI-BASED SPENDING SEQUENCE, ILLUSTRATING THE GOLDEN GROWTH CURVE

Note to the mathematically disinclined: You do not need to review this information in order to successfully do the Millionaire's MAP.™

SPENDING AMOUNT	100	100	200	300	500	800	1,300	2,100	3,400	5,500	8,900	14,400	23,300	37,700	61,000	98,700	159,700	258,400	418,100	676,500	1,094,600	2,865,600 = TOTAL AMOUNT SPENT OVER 21 DAYS
DAY	1	2	3	4	5	6	7	8	9	10	11	12	13	14	15	16	17	18	19	20	21	

Please note: Graph is not to scale.

The Millionaire's MAP gradually growing spending curve, based on starting Day One with $100. This unique, increasing spending pattern reflects the Fibonacci Sequence, Nature's Golden Growth Code for maximum efficiency and success. After Day Two, each successive day's Spending Amount is always the sum total of the previous two day's amounts. In the graph above for example, Day 6 ($800) is simply the combined sum of Day 5 ($500) and Day 4 ($300).

The key is to start the process with an amount that would be comfortable for you to go out and spend today on anything you want to or need, without feeling stressed. If you feel like starting the process with a higher amount than $100, you'd simply ADD a zero to the end of each spending amount, for example $100 becomes $1,000; $200 becomes $2,000, and so on. If you feel like starting the process with a lower amount than $100, you'd simply SUBTRACT a zero from the end of each spending amount, for example $100 becomes $10; $200 becomes $20, and so on.

The important thing to remember is that your Day One Spending Amount must always begin with a ONE followed only by ZEROS, regardless of whether your Day One Spending Amount is $10, $100, $1000 or $10,000. Your Day Two Spending Amount is always exactly the same as Day One. On the third day you combine Days One and Two to start The Millionaire's MAP golden growth spending curve, as in the example above.

The beginning is the most important part.

Plato

DAY 1
CONSCIOUS SPENDING

The Millionaire's MAP is a game that fuses the power of your imagination with the science of purposeful design. It's a process for attracting abundance, wealth and good fortune. It follows the fascinating Fibonacci Sequence, named after the greatest mathematician of the Middle Ages, Leonardo Fibonacci of Pisa. This ubiquitous, magical Sequence has captivated mankind since its discovery early in the 13th century. In an added twist, the infinite Fibonacci Sequence reflects the Golden Ratio—the master design code of the universe. More on this tomorrow.

Today is Day One of your Millionaire's MAP. According to the rules of the game, yesterday you had no extra money to spend—zero dollars. To begin today, imagine that you've just been given $100 to spend on anything, in any way you need or want. You can also start today with a lower (e.g. $10) or higher figure (e.g. $1000) if you like. The key is to start with an initial amount that's within your present comfort zone, within the simple "launch" guidelines of the Golden Growth Code. See the Spending Graph on the opposite page for details.

What you do with this money is entirely up to you. You can spend it all in one place or spend it on many things. You can pay bills with it, give it away, put it in the bank, make investments with it or purchase anything you wish. There is no one looking over your shoulder. No one to judge your spending choices. While the money you are given exists in the workshop of your mind, to get maximum benefit from the game you will need to FEEL as if it is REAL. The game is designed to upgrade your beliefs and attitudes around wealth and abundance in general. The bridge to this upgrade is the unlimited power of your imagination, focused through the conscious spending formula in this workbook.

Remember, your subconscious mind cannot tell the difference between things envisioned deep in your imagination and the "real" thing. The Millionaire's MAP process is like a virtual-reality gym, where you get to "pump up" and sculpt your expanded, wealthier future. It gives you great practice in living in the flow of increasing abundance. Once you've decided how to spend your daily money allotment, you'll make a few notes on the accompanying spending record page. There you'll record the amounts allocated to each item. At the bottom of each spending record page is a space where you can jot down any insights. Though this part is optional, it's a powerful way to deepen your experience and amplify the process. Write down anything you've learned about yourself and your relationship to money. This brief journal will record, day by day, your transformation.

MILLIONAIRE'S TIP

If starting your Millionaire's Map
with $100 is not challenging enough,
start with $1,000 (remember to *add* a
zero to each new day's amount here in
the book.) If starting with $100 feels
too challenging today, start with $10
(remember to *delete* a zero from each
new day's amount here in the book.)
Either way, be sure to follow the same
1,1,2,3,5,8… formula of increase for each
day. The key is that the spending
amount chosen for Day 1 must begin
with a 1 followed only by zeros.
No matter which amount you start with—
$10, $100, $1000 or even $10,000—
the process is equally powerful.

Today's Date

/ /

SPENDING RECORD

1

DAY ONE

Your total funds to
spend in full today is

$100

Today you receive $100 to spend. Jot down your items and their amounts.

No.	Items	Amount
	Total	**$100**

DAY
1

Insights from today's spending (optional):

_____

_____

_____

The Golden Proportion is a scale of proportions which makes the bad difficult [to produce] and the good easy.

Albert Einstein,
in a letter to Divine Code
Architect Le Corbusier

Geometry has two great treasures. One is the theorem of Pythagoras, the other, the division of a line into extreme and mean [Golden] ratio. The first we may compare to a measure of gold; the second we may name a precious jewel.

Johannes Kepler,
formulator of the Laws
of Planetary Motion

DAY 2
THE INFINITE FIBONACCI SEQUENCE

The process that became The Millionaire's MAP had been brewing in my mind for some time. I had heard and often thought about the idea of spending money in the workshop of my imagination—and even on paper—to invite greater abundance into my life. The premise was usually quite simple. For example, on the first day, you'd spend a certain amount of money, perhaps $100, on anything you wanted. Each following day, you'd spend double the previous day's amount. The problem was, I never actually put pen to paper and tried it. Somehow the doubling formula just didn't feel right to me. One day as I was examining my procrastination, I found that by doubling each day (e.g., $100, $200, $400, $800, $1600, $3200...), the resulting spending curve quickly got very steep. I played with a calculator and discovered that, by the end of the first month, I'd end up spending over $50 billion dollars in one day. This seemed a bit unrealistic to me—like too much too soon. So I dropped the idea and went about my life.

Some years later, with the idea occasionally popping into my mind, I had a flash of inspiration. "Instead of doubling your money each day," I said to myself, "Why not try using the Fibonacci Sequence?" In the magical Fibonacci Sequence of 0, 1, 1, 2, 3, 5, 8, 13, 21..., each successive number is the sum of the previous two. This is the formula for an infinite growth spiral that grows from within itself. Intriguingly, the ratio of any two successive Fibonacci numbers always approaches the Golden Ratio: 1.618..., also known as the Divine Proportion, Divine Code or simply Phi. It has been known since ancient times as the ubiquitous Master Code of growth, beauty, unity and transformation. This magic code describes and guides everything from the spiral of the Milky Way to the curl of ocean waves to the structure, growth, movement and behavior of plants, animals and humans, right down to our DNA. It even plays a vital role in Dan Brown's book *The Da Vinci Code*, one of the bestselling novels of all time.

The Fibonacci Sequence and associated Golden Ratio was one of the buried treasures of knowledge I had carried in the back of my mind since childhood. I knew I was on to something here. I immediately realized that the Fibonacci Sequence provided the ideal exponential growth spiral for the process which became The Millionaire's MAP. My procrastination dissolved in that instant. I knew it would work and had to try it myself. You are now experiencing the same process.

MILLIONAIRE'S TIP

Set aside at least five relaxed
minutes daily to add to your Millionaire's
MAP. I made the process my morning
ritual, and it became something
I eagerly looked forward to. Sometimes
I would make a special trip to my favorite
cafe to relax and write my daily entry
over a mocha latte. It's a fun way
to start your day.

Today's Date

/ /

SPENDING RECORD

2

DAY TWO

Your total funds to
spend in full today is

$100

Today you receive $100 to spend. Jot down your items and their amounts.

No.	Items	Amount
Total		$100

Insights from today's spending (optional):

_____

_____

_____

Leonardo Fibonacci of Pisa (c. 1170–1250).

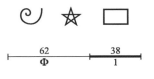

0, 1, 1, 2, 3, 5, 8, 13...

The five facets of the
Divine Code: The Golden Spiral,
Star, Rectangle; Golden Ratio
and Fibonacci Sequence.

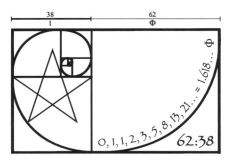

The Divine Code glyph, integrating
the five primary facets, as above.

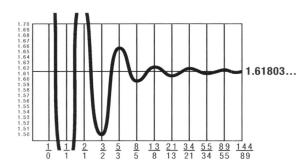

1.61803...

The Divine Code Pulse Graph, showing the
Fibonacci Sequence/Ratios forever zeroing-in
on the elusive Golden Ratio 1.61803...
As the numbers in the sequence get bigger,
the (Golden) ratio between them gets forever
finer, e.g., 34÷21 = 1.61904; 55÷34 = 1.61764;
89÷55 = 1.61818...

0
123456789
.

The Fibonacci Trinity:
• Zero
• The Hindu/Arabic Numbers
• The Decimal Point

Nature's Path of Least Resistance and Maximum Performance follows the Golden Mean.

Dr. Ron Sandler, Consistent Winning

DAY 3
THE GENIUS FROM PISA

The Golden Growth/Divine Code was greatly advanced in the 12th century by one of history's greatest yet forgotten mathematicians, Leonardo Fibonacci of Pisa. During his travels in Africa and the Near East with his father, young Fibonacci learned of three other mathematical elements which, once introduced to the Western world, forever transformed commerce, science and society. Fibonacci introduced:

1) Hindu/Arabic numerals: 1, 2, 3, 4..., which replaced Roman numerals: I, II, III, IV...
2) the decimal system.
3) the symbol, concept and name for Zero.

These three monumental contributions to the world form the Fibonacci Trinity.

Through this trinity, Fibonacci also introduced the mysterious, infinite sequence of numbers that bears his name: 0, 1, 1, 2, 3, 5, 8, 13, 21... From this magic sequence can be derived the Golden Ratio, the infinite growth-from-within code found throughout nature and the universe. This is the ubiquitous code behind the seen and unseen worlds. If there is such a thing as "God's Code" the Fibonacci Sequence and associated Golden Ratio/Divine Code would have to be it.

The Divine Code has fascinated geniuses through the centuries, from Plato to Da Vinci to Kepler. When Albert Einstein learned of it at 12 it had a profound effect on him. Leonardo Da Vinci and astronomer Johannes Kepler were similarly affected. In current times, Dr. Murray Gell-Mann, Nobel Prize-winner and pioneer of quark and chaos theory, told me that he remembered learning of the Fibonacci Sequence when he was five, and how much it fascinated him. Dr. Karl Pribram, acclaimed neurophysiologist and researcher of the brain's holographic nature, shared a similar story. As noted earlier, the Fibonacci Sequence also plays a key, appropriate role (as the secret access code to a vital Swiss bank safe deposit box) in Dan Brown's phenomenal best-seller *The Da Vinci Code*.

I first learned of the Fibonacci Sequence/Divine Code when I was 13. Ever since then I've been on a quest to unlock its secrets and apply it practically. It is also the subject of the book I authored with Dr. Robert Friedman, *The Divine Code of Da Vinci, Fibonacci, Einstein & YOU*. The Millionaire's MAP elegantly incorporates the Divine Code's principle of exponential growth into its structure and practice. It brings the infinite power of Nature's Golden Growth Code right into your hands.

MILLIONAIRE'S TIP

You may want to keep this process
to yourself, initially. For many, this
seems the best way to maintain good
focus while supporting a new wealth
growth spiral. Share the process with
others when the time feels right.

Today's Date

/ /

SPENDING RECORD

3

DAY THREE

Your total funds to
spend in full today is

$200

Today you receive $200 to spend. Jot down your items and their amounts.

No.	Items	Amount
Total		**$200**

Insights from today's spending (optional):

_____

_____

_____

Thinking big makes life a lot easier and a lot more fun.
It also makes profits more probable.

Richard Carlson, Ph.D.
Don't Worry, Make Money

DAY 4
UPGRADE YOUR FUTURE

The Millionaire's MAP is designed to upgrade your Life/Wealth Operating System. This in turn enhances your opportunities and upgrades your future into more of what you want it to be.

The good news is, you already possess the necessary hardware and software within you to run The Millionaire's MAP program successfully. Its underlying Fibonacci growth formula actually mirrors the very structure and function of your body, mind and emotions. This natural resonance factor is a key reason why the process works so powerfully to upgrade your attitudes and beliefs on many levels. Spending money on paper according to the Fibonacci Sequence is like a secret password that allows you to access and activate your greater potentials. Because it's also an exercise in unlimited imagination, it directly influences and lifts other areas in your life as well. As the popular saying goes, "A rising tide lifts all boats." The simple game that is The Millionaire's MAP supports you to:

❖ Experience creativity, fun, freedom and magic around money, spending and wealth growth
❖ Gain greater clarity about your most important life values
❖ Practice dealing with larger and larger sums of money, which you may not currently possess
❖ Upgrade your mindset from one of scarcity to one of growing cash flow and abundance

As you play the game, you will consciously upgrade your ability to attract greater wealth and abundance into your life. The process helps you to naturally remove old mental blocks and limiting thought patterns, which may have hindered you from attracting and enjoying greater abundance in the past. The secret is simple: You must first open your mind and heart to greater abundance, if you hope to create and allow it in your life. The power comes from exercising your infinite imagination, with Nature's Golden Growth Code as your coach and guide. It's time to pump it up!

MILLIONAIRE'S TIP

Each subsequent day's spending
amount is always the combined
sum of the previous two days.
This formula is Nature's code
for building a harmonious,
expanding golden spiral—
a new wealth growth curve.

Today's Date

/   /

SPENDING RECORD
4
DAY FOUR

Your total funds to
spend in full today is
$300

Today you receive $300 to spend. Jot down your items and their amounts.

No.	Items	Amount
Total		**$300**

DAY
4

Insights from today's spending (optional):

_____

_____

_____

What you really know is possible in your heart is possible…
What we imagine in our minds becomes our world.

Dr. Masaru Emoto, The Hidden Messages In Water

DAY 5
A MAGIC PROCESS

This book can transform your life. I say this with confidence because the simple, original 21-step process you are beginning has dramatically transformed mine. It increased my appreciation of the power latent within me. I continue to be delighted and intrigued with the ways it stretches my imagination and enhances my life.

I took my first 21-day test flight of The Millionaire's MAP several years ago. I did exactly what you're doing now. Within ninety days of completing the process my income more than tripled, in an exciting way I had not foreseen. Additionally, the process led me to begin actively using much more of my knowledge and talents. From that point on, my financial life began a new upward spiral. Other areas of my life also began a positive transformation, which continues to this day. I have growing confidence in my financial dealings. I am accomplishing projects that, years ago, seemed like mere dreams. I also enjoy increasing clarity, confidence and enjoyment around the meaning and purpose of my life. Just as my financial bank account has grown, so has my life and spiritual bank accounts. In these last two, the balance of confidence, excitement and gratitude grows and compounds daily.

As I look back today, I can see that doing my first Millionaire's MAP was one of the clearest points where my life took a deliberate and dramatically abundant turn. It's like tracing the ripples in a pond back to the "splash point" where the pebble hit the water. By simply filling in your daily spending record, you are now throwing your own "Millionaire's Pebble" into the pond of your life. The ripples resulting from these seemingly small, daily actions can grow into great waves of wealth and abundance.

MILLIONAIRE'S TIP

Whether you want to use your daily
money to reduce your credit card debt
or make a down payment on a Caribbean
cruise, you decide what to spend your
money on. The only condition is,
you must spend all of each day's
money allotment on that day.

Today's Date

/ /

5

DAY FIVE

Your total funds to
spend in full today is

$500

DAY
5

Today you receive $500 to spend. Jot down your items and their amounts.

No.	Items	Amount
Total		$500

Insights from today's spending (optional):

_____

_____

_____

31

YOU WIN!

You can't win any game unless
you are ready to win.

Connie Mack

DAY 6
SOME INITIAL RESULTS

In addition to myself, this process has also benefited the many people I have shared it with. My experiences and theirs first led me to design and lead The Millionaire's MAP workshop, and then to capture the heart of the process in this book.

My friend Peter was once a struggling actor in Los Angeles. Working odd jobs to stay afloat while pursuing his acting dream, he often skated on the financial edge. Then he tried The Millionaire's MAP. Within 45 days he was offered—seemingly out of the blue—his first national television commercial, demonstrating fitness equipment for Sears. You may have seen him on television, working out on the Nordic Track. Peter ended up earning many thousands of dollars in residuals from that one commercial. Shortly thereafter, Peter was offered and accepted a job working directly for a Hollywood legend. He now regularly interacts with mega-millionaires, while honing his own investment and wealth-building skills.

Many people—even those doing work they enjoy—can be held back from greater abundance by a scarcity or "just enough" mindset. This is often not conscious. With their scarcity program playing over and over in their minds, it can be difficult for these people to allow abundance to flow into their lives. The daily spending exercises in The Millionaire's MAP will help replace that scarcity mindset with a growing readiness and magnetism for increasing abundance.

MILLIONAIRE'S TIP

Don't judge or criticize yourself
for what you choose to spend your
money on. Let go and play! The secret
is to feel yourself spending your daily
cash, and enjoying the process as if it
were real. Have fun, and remember:
There's even more money coming
your way tomorrow!

Today's Date

/ /

6

DAY SIX

Your total funds to
spend in full today is

$800

DAY
6

Today you receive $800 to spend. Jot down your items and their amounts.

No.	Items	Amount
Total		$800

Insights from today's spending (optional):

_____

_____

_____

35

Imagination is everything. It is the preview of life's coming attractions.

Albert Einstein

.

DAY 7
IMAGINATION:
PASSPORT TO PROSPERITY

"Imagination is more important than knowledge," said Albert Einsten; "I never made any of my greatest discoveries through the process of rational thinking alone."

I've always felt this quote was loaded with meaning. Imagination is a gift we are all born with. Throughout childhood we have it in joyful abundance. Yet, for many, it slowly fades as we move through the regimented maze of modern schooling and societal conditioning. By the time many people become adults, their powers of unlimited imagination have often been greatly diminished. Yet imagination is the compass that guides us toward our purpose. It awakens our natural gifts and talents. Simply put, a healthy imagination holds a vital key to our brightest future.

From a young age, Albert Einstein was not a fan of conventional schooling. He felt that it extinguished the bright light of creativity, imagination and genius we are all born with. Einstein instinctively understood that the blueprint behind modern schooling was actually based on the Prussian Military model, whose primary aim was to turn out "good soldiers" who follow orders and don't exercise their imagination. Not surprisingly, the man who many consider to be the greatest genius who ever lived did his best to protect and rigorously exercise his own imagination. The preservation of Einstein's unlimited imagination was largely due to his own self-education process, which often confounded his teachers.

Fortunately, no one ever loses the power present within their imagination. As noted earlier, some key functions of imagination are to help you discover your purpose and shape your future. One fascinating and little-known fact about Einstein is his discovery at age 12 of the Fibonacci Sequence—the Golden Growth Code at the heart of The Millionaire's MAP. This discovery ignited young Einstein's imagination about the structure and order of the universe. One could say that Einstein's most famous equation, the Theory of Relativity ($e=MC2$), was inspired by the same golden, universal formula underlying this book. This is the same formula that is at the heart of the genius of Nature and all creation. The Millionaire's MAP process is an enjoyable, almost addictive way to ignite and renew your imagination. It's your passport to prosperity and purpose, your first-class ticket to a more expanded life.

MILLIONAIRE'S TIP

In your imagination, really see, feel, hear, sense and enjoy whatever you purchase, even if just during the moments you're writing it down. What would it be like to actually *have* what you've spent your money on? *Imagine that...*

Today's Date

/ /

SPENDING RECORD

7

DAY SEVEN

Your total funds to
spend in full today is
$1,300

Today you receive $1,300 to spend. Jot down your items and their amounts.

No.	Items	Amount
	Total	**$1,300**

Insights from today's spending (optional):

_____

_____

_____

Unlike raw material and products,
information is the basis for two-way
shared transactions.

When I share valuable information with
you, I also get to keep it. It serves us both.

Information grows in value exponentially
the more it is shared...

Harland Cleveland

DAY 8
PATTERNED INFORMATION = WEALTH

I wrote this book to concisely share the secrets of The Millionaire's MAP with you. I did this because I think we can all benefit from an increase of abundance and magic in our lives. All the books I write and the workshops I lead have one major purpose: to help people find deeper meaning and more fulfillment and success in their lives. The Millionaire's MAP can launch and guide your dreams of a greater future. It also prepares a runway on which your dreams can land. It surfaces information that adds growing value to all of your tomorrows. Each day provides priceless practice in handling and enjoying growing wealth.

Harlan Cleveland, friend and eminent futurist, was among the first to articulate the unique wealth-building power of information in this age of technology and rapid change. Harlan points out that information is the true currency of our time, replacing labor, materials and even money as the prime medium of value. This is because whenever we exchange labor, materials or money for something we lose those items in the exchange. This sets up a classic win-lose dynamic. However, the sharing of information sets up a magical win-win situation. That's because when we share information with others, we also get to keep it as well. And here's perhaps the best news behind this principle: the more valuable the information we share with others is, the more its worth grows over time. An added potential bonus is that what we share with others—free of expectations—tends to come back to us at some point, often multiplied.

The strategic perspective that results from recognizing meaningful (yet often hidden) patterns within pieces of information is itself a priceless commodity. Pattern recognition, as this skill is called, is an easily developed skill for enhanced intelligence and success. Through The Millionaire's MAP process, you get to create and explore new patterns of gold-nugget information and experiences. Simply put, The Millionaire's MAP journey offers you precisely patterned and sequenced information that will help you create a golden future.

MILLIONAIRE'S TIP

Suspend any doubt, worry or present
financial challenges while you practice
your wealth-building Millionaire's MAP.
Be confident and strong as you spend
your daily cash amount. Reach for your
dreams, and they will reach for you.

Today's Date

___/___/___

SPENDING RECORD
8
DAY EIGHT

Your total funds to
spend in full today is
$2,100

Today you receive $2,100 to spend. Jot down your items and their amounts.

No.	Items	Amount
Total		$2,100

DAY 8

Insights from today's spending (optional):

_____

_____

_____

The Deming Prize, Japan's highest
award for quality excellence since 1951.

85% of the results are in the first 15% of the process.

Dr. W. Edwards Deming (attributed)

DAY 9
DR. DEMING: EINSTEIN OF QUALITY & SUCCESS

A key mentor of mine is American quality legend Dr. W. Edwards Deming. His genius continues to have a profound impact on the world and in my life and work. Deming is the man the Japanese credit with lifting them from the ashes of WWII, leading them to become the world's second-largest economy and undisputed quality leader. The "Deming DNA" is a vital factor in the worldwide success of companies such as Toyota, Canon, Harley-Davidson and Proctor & Gamble, to name just a few. I call Dr. Deming the Einstein of quality and success.

Dr. Deming defined true wisdom as knowledge that allows you to better predict future outcomes and performance. Enhancing one's predictive ability is, in his view, a vital priority for all leaders and managers. It applies equally to anyone wanting to achieve lasting success. One of the keys to being a better predictor is having dependable, quality systems. A quality system is simply a series of visible, interconnected steps pointing towards a desired outcome or aim. It has a beginning, a middle and a predictable result. Deming noted that setting goals without having the system and methods in place to predictably achieve them accomplishes little or nothing. A key reason I developed The Millionaire's MAP was to create a simple yet powerful system to help make real what I wanted in my life—and keep me focused on it as I progressed.

Everyone needs the ability to be a better predictor. We can all benefit from knowledge that allows us to better predict future performance and outcomes. I've researched, refined and taught predictive tools and strategies to organizations and individuals for many years now. It's a passion for me. You are now beginning to make long-range plans, to predict what you want to do with the increasing amounts of money available to you in this process. The Millionaire's MAP has an uncanny ability to plant and nurture your desires for a more prosperous and exciting future. It will support your ability to predict, anticipate and sculpt your future to the scale of your imagination.

MILLIONAIRE'S TIP

Start expecting and noticing all signs
of abundance around you, no matter
how small. Pick up coins on the sidewalk.
Welcome unexpected gifts, new clients
or accounts, or a new, more lucrative job
offer. Expect rewarding surprises!

Today's Date

/ /
_____

SPENDING RECORD

9

DAY NINE

Your total funds to
spend in full today is

$3,400

Today you receive $3,400 to spend. Jot down your items and their amounts.

No.	Items	Amount
Total		**$3,400**

Insights from today's spending (optional):

_____

_____

_____

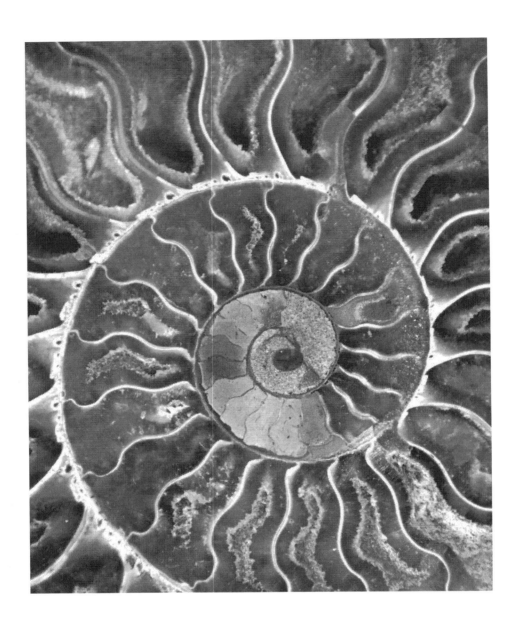

Cross' Universal Law #3:
Whatever you APPRECIATE (regularly focus your heart and mind on, value), APPRECIATES (grows, like assets in a bank).

Matthew Cross

DAY 10
THE MAGIC OF APPRECIATION

Sometimes the effects of The Millionaire's MAP process start in seemingly small ways. A few days after starting her first Millionaire's MAP, my friend Patricia looked down as she was getting into her car—and saw a crisp new $50 bill on the sidewalk. She bent down and picked it up, smiling to herself. This was the first time she had found anything larger than a $1 bill. Like all of us, every now and then she would find a penny on the ground. Yet the timing of this particular event seemed like a strong coincidence to her. She felt a sense of affirmation about the process and a new sense of potential and possibility in her life.

Paying attention to and appreciating initial signs, however small, is part of the fun and power of The Millionaire's MAP. When you learn to recognize and truly appreciate the *small,* you set the stage to receive and enjoy the *all.* The secret is regular appreciation—focused, heartfelt gratitude—for the many gifts we have today, both the small and the large, as well as those to come. The simple magic of regular appreciation unlocks the vault of our highest aspirations and potential.

MILLIONAIRE'S TIP

For some, the obvious signs of
impending wealth may start small and
subtly, like finding more pennies than
usual on the sidewalk. For others, it can
seem as if a great waterfall of prosperity
begins to flow into your life. Either way,
know that the universe is just itching
to fill your life bank account with
wealth and abundance.

Today's Date

/ /

10

DAY TEN

Your total funds to
spend in full today is

$5,500

Today you receive $5,500 to spend. Jot down your items and their amounts.

No.	Items	Amount
	Total	**$5,500**

DAY
10

Insights from today's spending (optional):

_____

_____

_____

Money is God in action.
Frederick J. Eikerenkoetter II
"Reverend Ike"

DAY 11
PLAYING THE GAME OF INCREASE

Years ago, my friend Gurumarka wanted a new car. Since moving to Europe he had mostly gotten around by bike and train. However, at the time his finances were a little tight to go and buy the new car he wanted outright. Soon after, he tried The Millionaire's MAP. Within two months of completing the process, one of his clients called him out of the blue and said:

> *"My sister-in-law just passed away and left us her car. We have no need for it and we know you are in the market for a car..."*

Before he could explain that he was not in a position to buy their car at that time, his client continued: "...and we would like to give it to you." They simply presented him with the car. At the time it was virtually new, with only 10,000 miles on it. He drove his new white Opel all over Europe for two years. I had the pleasure of riding in it whenever I visited him. Recently the same client was about to trade in their beautiful charcoal-grey Mercedes for a new one. Instead they called Gurumarka. Now he drives a Mercedes.

MILLIONAIRE'S TIP

Start paying attention to all the wealth
around you. Train your eyes to notice and
appreciate abundance wherever you are.
Notice shiny new cars, well-dressed people
and opulent homes. Delight in your
wealth of imagination and freedom, the
vast supply of fresh air to breathe and
the smiles of children. True wealth is
everywhere you look, in every
moment. Breathe it in.

Today's Date

/ /

SPENDING RECORD

11

DAY ELEVEN

Your total funds to
spend in full today is

$8,900

Today you receive $8,900 to spend. Jot down your items and their amounts.

No.	Items	Amount
	Total	$8,900

Insights from today's spending (optional):

_____

_____

_____

I was constantly told
and challenged to live
my life as a warrior.

As a warrior, you
assume responsibility
for yourself. The warrior
humbles himself.

And the warrior learns
the power of giving...

God has given me
the ability, the rest
is up to me.

Believe. Believe. Believe...

———————

Your life is a gift from the
Creator. Your gift back to
the Creator is what you do
with your life.

Billy Mills,
Oglala Lakota Sioux
Warrior and
10k Olympic Gold
Medalist, 1964

Billy Mills and the author in 2004

DAY 12
BILLY MILLS: A WARRIOR'S WILL TO WIN

Billy Mills, a member of the Oglala Sioux Tribe, grew up on the Pine Ridge Indian Reservation in South Dakota. His Lakota name, Makcoe The'la, means "love your country," more traditionally translated as "respects the earth." Billy grew up in poverty and was orphaned at age 12, when he was sent to an Indian boarding school. He kept a positive life focus by taking up running. After building his natural talent and winning many races throughout high school and college, Billy joined the Marines and dreamed of one day competing in the Olympics. He invested hundreds of hours while in the Marines, training for his golden dream. Billy demonstrated the power of the saying that "the will to win means nothing without the will to train."

Billy was so focused on his dream that he made the USA Track & Field Team in two events: the 10,000 meter (6.2 mile) run and the marathon, for the 1964 Olympic Games in Tokyo, Japan. Yet as a near-total unknown he was thought to have little chance of winning a medal. In fact, the shoe sponsor of the USA Track & Field team was so convinced Billy wouldn't medal, a manager refused to issue him shoes for the Olympic 10k race. Billy ended up running in the championship race in borrowed shoes. Only after the owner of the shoe company was interviewed was Billy issued shoes to compete in. They became the first pair of track shoes Billy owned outright.

In the 10k final, Mills surprised nearly everyone by staying with the lead runners throughout the race, including the then-current 10k world record holder. Although he was elbowed into the outer lanes in the last lap, Billy sprinted like a Cheetah past the two front-runners in the final 100 yards, winning the race by 4/10ths of a second. Billy's astonishing achievement is still considered by many to be the most dramatic upset in Olympic history. All his thousands of hours of training culminated in the final moments of his historic victory. The last lap is one of the most electrifying athletic events on film. Billy's life is also the subject of the film *Running Brave*, starring Robby Benson.

Billy remains the only American to win the Olympic 10k. He said he kept his focus by visualizing himself as an Olympic champion, repeating to himself whenever he fell a little behind, "One more try, one more try!" As he neared the finish line, his inner chant changed to "I can win, I can win!" Today, Billy is a devoted family man, acclaimed motivational speaker, author (*Lessons of a Lakota*, with Nicholas Sparks) and founder of Running Strong for American Indian Youth. He is a warrior of the spirit and a champion of the infinite potential within everyone.

The Millionaire's MAP is your personal wealth and life purpose training arena. You train for your dreams of a more abundant life by affirming your positive focus, even if it sometimes feels you must come from behind. As Billy Mills says, "Every Passion has its Destiny."

MILLIONAIRE'S TIP

Buddha said: "We are shaped by
our thoughts; we become what we think."
What are your thoughts about more money
and abundance flowing into your life?
Will you be ready and able to enjoy greater
wealth when it arrives? Notice any doubts
or limiting beliefs that may have come up
around this idea—and then throw them
right into an imaginary recycling bin.
You don't need them anymore.

Today's Date

___ / ___ / ___

SPENDING RECORD
12
DAY TWELVE

Your total funds to
spend in full today is
$14,400

Today you receive $14,400 to spend. Jot down your items and their amounts.

No.	Items	Amount
		Total **$14,400**

Insights from today's spending (optional):

_____

_____

_____

What you already know is merely a departure point.
Keorapetse Kgositsile

DAY 13
BAMBOO & THE ART OF LOOKING DEEPER

You've probably heard stories about people who bought a $10 print at a flea market, just for the nice wooden frame. Then, looking deeper, they discovered that a priceless document or painting was stashed behind the cheap print—perhaps a forgotten sketch by Picasso or a lost original copy of the U.S. Constitution.

The secret to successfully using The Millionaire's MAP is simple. It's the practice of looking deeper into the process of focused imagination with feeling. On the surface, the process of spending money on paper (tuned to the Fibonacci Sequence) may seem no more significant than playing any other solitary game. Yet as you seriously engage in The Millionaire's MAP and let your imagination soar—as you feel what it would be like to really have and spend your daily cash allotment—a priceless transformation is happening within you, beneath the surface. You are opening the door to the limitless abundance that's all around every one of us in every moment.

The valuable, growing effects of The Millionaire's MAP process are often hidden inside of you at first. The process is similar to what happens when bamboo seeds are first planted. After planting, the bamboo farmer carefully waters and protects the seeds. At the end of the first year, there's no sign of any growth. The farmer patiently continues the process of caring for the seeds over year two. Still no sign of growth. Then comes year three. Nothing. Not even a tiny sprout. Then, at the end of year three—boom! the bamboo shoots out of the ground, growing up to eighteen feet in one year. And just as with a bamboo seed, or in how a tiny acorn can grow into a mighty oak tree, the seeds you plant daily in your unlimited imagination can yield fantastic, abundant results over time.

MILLIONAIRE'S TIP

Honor the money that's in your life right
now. For example, keep your dollar bills
neatly folded instead of crumpled up.
Treat the money in your life with gratitude,
respect and love, and it will surely grow.
Lastly, honor this moment and really
let yourself enjoy today's spending.
This moment holds enormous power.

Today's Date

/ /

Your total funds to
spend in full today is
$23,300

Today you receive $23,300 to spend. Jot down your items and their amounts.

No.	Items	Amount
Total		**$23,300**

DAY
13

Insights from today's spending (optional):

_____

_____

_____

OPTIONAL BREAK DAYS

NOTE: Feel free to skip this section and continue with Day 14 on page 73.

Sometimes, around the 13th day of The Millionaire's MAP process (note that 13 is a lucky Fibonacci number) some people need a break. It can get a little overwhelming for some, managing and spending all this money day after day. Around this time, some might even be tempted to give up completely. If any of the above is the case with you, I suggest you go ahead and take a nice break. Come back to the workbook with a fresh perspective in a few days.

Don't worry—the process will wait for you. It never goes stale. In fact, sometimes stepping back actually *amplifies* the process. I call this the catapult factor: Catapults always have to pull back (like taking a break) before they shoot their payload forward. For many people the 24 hours between each daily spending exercise is enough of a "catapult break." For others, a break of several days around Day 13 may be in order. It can allow you to adjust to and integrate your new abundance mindset.

Of course if you're still raring to go you can skip the following optional break pages and get ready to spend your Day 14 allotment of $37,000 on page 73. Yet if you feel like you need a break, take one. If this is the case, I recommend trying a Fibonacci break—one that lasts for 1, 2, 3 or maybe even 5 days before resuming the process.

If you do choose to take a break and you'd like something different and fun to do during your break time, following here are three great exercises. The first is a Wealth Collage; the second, as inspired by actor Jim Carrey, is called A Check From the Universe. The third and final exercise is the TimeMAP, a process I developed years ago for creating a visual matrix linking past, present and future.

Giving and receiving are one in truth.
A Course in Miracles

OPTIONAL BREAK DAY 1
THE COLLAGE OF WEALTH

Instructions for Break Day 1

On a large piece of paper or posterboard, create a Wealth Collage. The way I do this is to simply gather (from magazines, newspapers, catalogues, etc.) photos of things I would like to possess or have access to, places I would like to visit or explore, settings in which I might like to work, people I would like to meet and spend time with—whatever represents, to me, great wealth, abundance and joy. You might also include gifts and symbols of your kindness to others. Prosperity always brings with it many opportunities to lift the world by acts of generosity and good will.

Take a little time collecting the initial images that best symbolize your coming prosperity. Don't hurry the process. A key thing to remember here is this: you don't need to have every last exact picture in hand in order to begin your wealth collage. Just get a good beginning set of cut-out pictures, even just 5 or 8, to start. You can also mix in single inspirational words or sentences you write down, print out or cut out from newspaper headlines, e.g., "winner," "the good life," "you did it!", "new millionaire," "the best," "true love found," "on top of the world," etc. You can also add a few favorite inspiring quotes.

Once your initial cut-outs are ready and spread out, you can begin your collage. With a glue stick, affix your chosen images to your large paper or poster board. Move them around until every item seems to be in a good place. When you're ready, you can glue or tape them into place. Hang your Wealth Collage somewhere prominent in your home. You might even add additional pictures, words or phrases to it from time to time. Every time you pass it, stop a moment and feel what it will be like to be living in your new world. Repeatedly feel it as if it is now—and it is.

OPTIONAL BREAK DAY 2
JIM CARREY'S $10 MILLION CHECK
FROM THE UNIVERSE

In the beginning of his career, Jim Carrey was a struggling actor living in his car. Around that time, he began the unique practice outlined here in a brief excerpt from a 1995 interview in *Entertainment Weekly Magazine:*

EW: We're just a few weeks from Thanksgiving 1995. That's when you post-dated a check to yourself for $10 million dollars. You were off by $10 million. [Carrey had just recently received a $20 million dollar movie offer] Why did you aim so low?

JC: I don't know (laughs.) When I wrote the $10 million dollar check [years before] it wasn't about the money; it was about working with the top people, for example the best directors.

EW: Did you write the check on one of your checking account checks?

JC: No, it was basically on a 3x5 card, but I wrote it like a check. If it had been on one of my checks, it would have been from me to me. This way it was from the universe, "for acting services rendered."

Carrey's approach was wonderfully simple: First, he would go to a high point overlooking the city of Los Angeles and clear any negative or limiting thoughts from his mind. Then, Jim would repeat to himself over and over again, as he pictured his ideal future: "I have many movie offers; I have a lot of wonderful directors wanting to work with me." He would feel it as if it were vibrantly real and rehearse it, over and over again in his heart and mind. Today of course, Jim Carrey is one of the most successful and beloved entertainers in the world. And the Universal Bank made good on his check—many times over.

You make your life; you think your life up...
Whatever you have the nerve to believe will actually happen.
Jim Carrey, USA Today; February 15, 2007

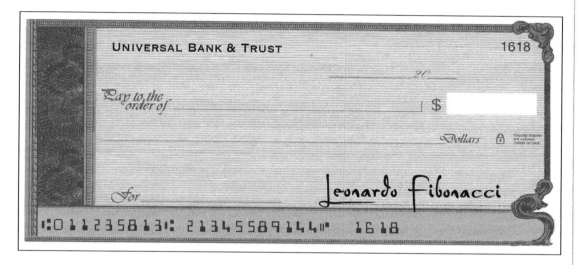

Try it. Follow Jim Carrey's technique as closely as you wish. Fill out the check above, payable to yourself in any amount you desire. Be outrageous! Go for millions!

Review your completed check often—ideally in a quiet place for 2–3 minutes, at least once a day—more if you wish. Imagine how it would feel and what you would do if this check was *really real*.

Most people see what is, and never see what can be.
Albert Einstein

OPTIONAL BREAK DAY 3
THE TIMEMAP PROCESS

When I turned 13, I began thinking seriously about my future. I wondered where my life would take me in the years ahead. I was becoming aware that the chapters of my childhood were slowly closing behind me. I remember wanting to capture the key events of growing up—where I'd been, what had shaped me, meaningful events—and blend them with my hopes and dreams for the future. I thought if I wrote down both my past and my future dreams on one page, my dreams would have a better chance of becoming real, since they'd be sharing the same paper with my real past.

Perhaps I could "remember" a more ideal future (and therefore better blueprint and invite it) just as easily as I could remember my past. After all, the word remember simply means "to call to mind or think of again." Perhaps there was a creative power in remembering, or calling to mind again, desired future life scenarios. I sensed great potential power in this idea of "remembering forward." It was during this period that I created the TimeMAP graph, a way to easily and visually chart the past and blueprint my ideal future. The process is now a key component in my Hoshin Success Compass workshops. I've also created many personal TimeMAP's in the years since that first one I did at age 13. They have proven to be an entertaining and enlightening way to honor what went before, gain better perspective on the present, and spark my imagination about the future. I offer you a condensed version of the TimeMAP here, as another supportive stepping stone on your journey. The whole process can take as little as 8 minutes.

To begin your TimeMAP, grab this book and some good pens (a few different colors are great) and find a quiet place where you won't be disturbed. Sit comfortably. Become aware of your breath. Gently slow and deepen it, breathing into your belly, as opposed to just your chest. Breathe out any stress or tension… Breathe in relaxation. After a few deep, relaxing breaths, close your eyes. Know that in this exercise you are safe and fully protected—only good and supportive things can touch you. Let your mind gently revisit your best memories, meaningful events and turning points in your past. Here are some suggested questions to get you started:

- ❖ What are some of your greatest personal triumphs?
- ❖ Where did you really shine, making yourself (and those close to you) proud?
- ❖ When did you blast through any limitations and touch your full potential?
- ❖ Where do you have positive, uplifting memories around money and wealth?
- ❖ Where have you given your support, wisdom or love and made a difference in someone's life?

Be a time traveler and allow yourself to go back in time and really be there again. Keep your breath relaxed and full, breathing into your belly. See, feel, hear, touch and taste those influential memories. No need to strain or try to remember every little detail. Just allow any important sights, sounds, feelings or general impressions to move gently through your mind. Don't worry that you'll forget any of it. Just trust that you'll easily remember whatever you need to.

Now, prepare to go back to your future. Leave the past behind and gently shift your focus forward. What are some of your aspirations and wild dreams? What in the future would make you dance on the rooftops and light up the world? *How would you live and give if you had no limitations?* Allow yourself to really fantasize. Let your imagination soar as you touch your highest dreams and feel the joy in your soul. Keep breathing deeply. After a few minutes, when it feels right, come back to the present. Open your eyes slowly and give yourself a few moments to get reoriented. Then, use your pen to fill in your top memories—both past and future—on your TimeMAP (example and TimeMAP on next page.) Simply fill in a few words or, at most, a short sentence for each entry. Select the date, as near as you can remember; if you're not sure, mark the ribbon of time with your best guess. Have fun with this and let it flow—don't try to be "perfect" or get every word just right. Just let the words flow quickly and note the approximate dates of events. Try for at least eight best past and five ideal future memories. Include symbols and different colors as you like. Make this process a game and have some fun with it.

When you're done, circle your top past and future entries, based on their meaning and how powerful they make you feel today. Study your choices and results. Note any interesting connections or patterns. This is a great opportunity to practice your pattern recognition skills. As with your wealth collage, consider making a copy of your completed TimeMAP and putting it up where you'll see it often. Let it remind you of the power in your past and the promise in your present, as you step into the magical future you've blueprinted on your TimeMAP.

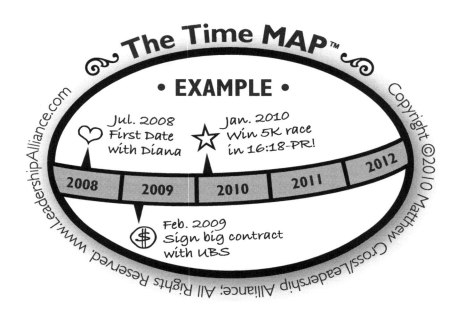

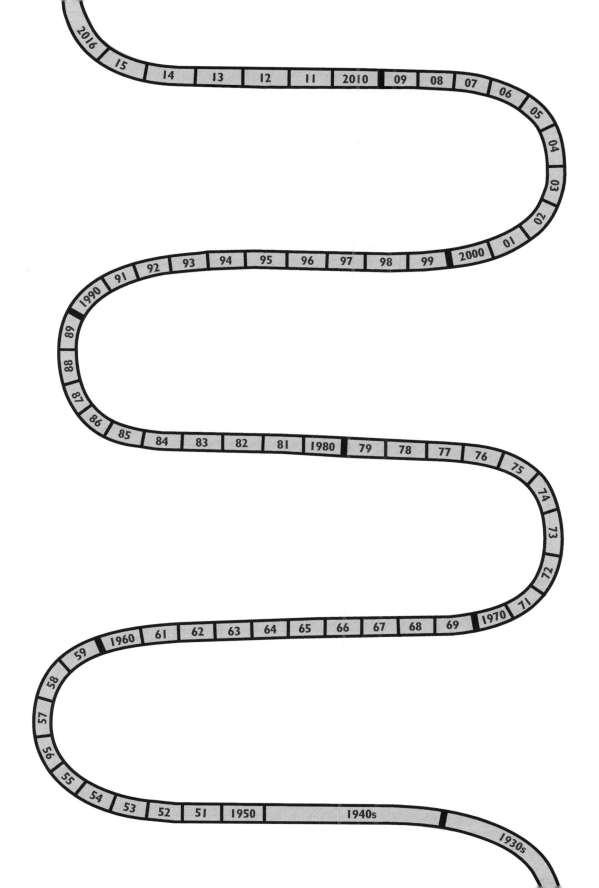

Some see things as they are and ask, "Why?"
I dream things that never were and ask, "Why not?"

Robert F. Kennedy,
adapted from George Bernard Shaw

DAY 14
FEEL THE JOY

Welcome back.

I trust you're refreshed and ready to charge ahead.

As mentioned earlier, a big key to the success of this game is for you to really feel and enjoy what it would be like to actually spend your daily allotment of money. That's one reason for the suggestion to capture a few personal observations each day, in the journal space below your spending record.

As you continue to move up your wealth growth spiral, use your imagination to see, hear, touch and especially feel the things you're spending your money on. Fully engaging all of your senses powerfully amplifies your imagination. For example: If you decided to buy a red Ferrari convertible, how would it feel to be holding the steering wheel, sitting in its comfortable seat, zooming along an open highway enjoying the beautiful sights, wind in your hair, hearing your favorite song playing above the purr of the engine? If you decided to buy a new home, what would it look like? Where would it be? How would it feel to stand in its front hall? What would you see as you looked around? Could you also taste any of your spending experiences? How would that gourmet candlelit dinner overlooking the Riviera with your sweetheart taste?

Imagine yourself talking to a best friend, explaining to him or her why you're making a purchase or giving a gift. Ask yourself: "What core values are driving me as I play this game of abundance and opportunity?" Are you investing? Are you being philanthropic? Do your purchases make you feel happy and strong? Would they please and delight others? Would you care? Allow yourself the freedom to spend your cash on things and experiences that will lift your world, and that of the people around you. The more you spend, the more you get to spend. The Universal Bank has unlimited funds and likes to finance big dreams. The bigger the better!

MILLIONAIRE'S TIP

What are your best memories of wealth?
In what situations have you felt wealthy?
Make a quick list of those times and
places, and write them on a 3 x 5 index
card. Keep the card where you can see
it every day. Remembering those times
and feelings adds power and speed
to your wealth journey.

Today's Date

/ /

Your total funds to
spend in full today is
$37,700

Today you receive $37,700 to spend. Jot down your items and their amounts.

No.	Items	Amount
Total		**$37,700**

DAY
14

Insights from today's spending (optional):

_____

_____

_____

Success comes from within,
not from without. It begins by
listening to your inner calling
and wisdom. What do you
truly value and enjoy?

What is your heart
trying to tell you?
Is there something
that you need
to pursue?

These are the
types of questions
that will put you on
your path toward
greatness.

Once on that path,
you will discover your
own unique way to make
the path an enormous
success and a great deal
of fun. The path will be clear
when you listen to your own
inner voice.

Richard Carlson, Ph.D.
Don't Worry, Make Money

DAY 15
THE ANCIENT TECHNOLOGY FOR CREATING MIRACLES

The Millionaire's MAP is about inviting and allowing abundant growth in all desired areas of your life—including, yet definitely not limited to, money and financial prosperity. This is where you liberate your Inner Life Millionaire. Increasing amounts of money are really just a metaphor you're using here, making it easy to count and track your expanding growth spiral.

As you spend increasing amounts of money in your imagination on the things, people and experiences that lift and delight you, you are sending a powerful message to your future. You are practicing having all that you want by feeling and enjoying it now. Practicing and having are not separate. Gregg Braden, author of *The God Code*, puts it this way: "Feeling and prayer are one in the same. When feeling and prayer are as one, when our heart and mind unite around our desires, we tap into an ancient technology for creating miracles in our lives."

I like to say that all of the things we want are actually created twice: first in our heart and mind, and then in our reality. The Millionaire's MAP is a custom workshop in which you design and plan a more abundant and fulfilling future. If you design and enjoy it well there, with focused daily feeling, it will surely come.

MILLIONAIRE'S TIP

Who are your role models when it comes
to wealth? Is there someone you know,
or know of, who seems to be living an
abundant, wealthy, healthy and balanced
life? Make it a point in the coming month
to spend some time with these kind of
people. If you don't know anyone who fits
this profile, find wealthy people to read
about, and learn from them.

Today's Date

_____ / _____ / _____

SPENDING RECORD

15

DAY FIFTEEN

Your total funds to
spend in full today is

$61,000

Today you receive $61,000 to spend. Jot down your items and their amounts.

No.	Items	Amount
	Total	$61,000

Insights from today's spending (optional):

_____

_____

_____

Matt Damon in 2001

Brendan Fraser and my
sister Jana

Matthew on the set

My sister Jana and me on
the set of the film *School Ties*

All the breaks you need in life wait within your imagination. Imagination is the workshop of your mind, capable of turning mind energy into accomplishment and wealth... Cherish your visions and your dreams as they are the children of your soul, the blueprints of your ultimate achievements.

Napoleon Hill

DAY 16

WRITE YOUR OWN SCRIPT:
A FEW WORDS WITH MATT DAMON

In the fall of 1991 I auditioned for a part in a movie, at the suggestion of my actor friend Peter. I ended up spending a month working on the film, along with Peter and my sister Jana. In one scene I was a prep school student; in another an alumnus; in the third, a maitre d'. Filming was on location near my home in Andover, Massachusetts. I had a great time on the set and got to experience first-hand the magic of movie making. It was particularly fascinating to watch how it all unfolded from the script. The script was the master blueprint that told everyone where to be, when to be there and with whom, what to do, the scenery—everything! The whole experience is one of my best memories.

The film, released by Paramount Pictures, is called *School Ties*. Its cast of then-unknown actors included Brendan Fraser, Matt Damon, Ben Affleck and Chris O'Donnell. In a break between filming scenes one day I had a conversation with Matt Damon. At the time he was a somewhat shy 21-year-old Harvard junior. I told him I thought he was a very talented actor. "You're really good," I said. Although his talent was abundantly obvious, he seemed perhaps a bit unsure of it at the time. Matt thanked me, yet I sensed that he wasn't totally certain that acting was his future. Nevertheless, he and his best friend Ben Affleck stuck with their dream of becoming successful actors. They later moved to Los Angeles to try their luck in Hollywood.

After years of B and C movie roles and offers Matt was getting discouraged. He'd almost had enough. So he began to write his own script, based on a short story he had written in school. When at one point he got stuck in the writing, Ben helped him. Together they wrote and starred in what became the hit Miramax film *Good Will Hunting,* which won them both an Oscar® for Best Original Screenplay in 1998. By doing what was in their hearts and imagination, and literally writing their own script, Matt and Ben sealed their destiny. Writing their own script was a powerful way of taking command of their lives and future.

In working through these pages you are writing your own script and creating your own future. You get to be the director, producer and star. So get ready to start filming your future. *Quiet on the set of your imagination...* ACTION!

MILLIONAIRE'S TIP

You're in the home stretch of the process now. Take stock of the *altitude of your attitude.* Your feelings are the compass that will guide you upward. Pay close attention to how you feel on this wealth journey and focus on those things that add lift, delight, direction and power.

Today's Date

/   /
_____

Your total funds to
spend in full today is
$98,700

Today you receive $98,700 to spend. Jot down your items and their amounts.

No.	Items	Amount
Total		**$98,700**

Insights from today's spending (optional):

_____

_____

_____

If you think you can't, why think?
Dee Hock
Founder and CEO Emeritus,
VISA International

DAY 17
YOUR PERSONAL TREASURE MAP

As far back as I can remember, I've always wanted to discover treasure—particularly buried treasure. As a child I devoured every book on lost (and found) treasure I could find. I imagined myself digging up great golden caches by cleverly solving clues on ancient treasure maps.

Years later, I came to realize that a vast treasure resides within the vaults of everyone's unlimited imagination. I've spent much of my life trying to figure out how to bring this treasure to the surface. My quest has led to the development and teaching of ways to uncover and activate the unique gifts—the priceless treasures—that reside within every one of us. What kind of treasures are you looking for in your life? The map and compass that will lead you to your true desires reside within your heart and imagination. It's not a coincidence that "Treasure Map" is another popular name for the Wealth Collage featured in the Optional Break Days section.

A simple theory behind this book is that what you would want to do with abundant sums of money reveals what you want to do with your life. Most of us have had little effective practice or training at managing our lives or our money. This book provides you with a treasure map for practicing abundant money management and growth. It also affords you the opportunity to discover what you want to do with money and your life, to make your life more abundant and fulfilling.

MILLIONAIRE'S TIP

What lies beyond money for you when
it comes to joy and fulfillment? I found
myself contemplating that question often
as I went through this process. You might
ask yourself the same question now.
It can enrich your spending patterns
in interesting ways.

Today's Date

/ /

SPENDING RECORD

17

DAY SEVENTEEN

Your total funds to
spend in full today is

$159,700

Today you receive $159,700 to spend. Jot down your items and their amounts.

No.	Items	Amount
	Total	$159,700

Insights from today's spending (optional):

_____

_____

_____

Dreams are illustrations... from the book
of your soul writing about you.
Marsha Norman

DAY 18
YOUR MILLIONAIRE GENES

Years ago my mom told me a wonderful story that her mother told her when she was young. At the end of WWI, mom's Uncle George made several trips by steamship (not a small undertaking in those days) to England to try to prove to the Bank of England that our family in the United States were rightful heirs to the Day Chocolate Company fortune. Her Uncle George's documentation was apparently incomplete and, unfortunately, all company papers at the factory were destroyed in enemy bombing raids during the war. If this story was true, and it could have been proven that we were indeed heirs of the great Day Chocolate Company fortune, none of our family would have ever had to work again.

I realized that merely thinking about having millions of dollars in my background suggested that I had the stuff of millionaires in my genes. It felt really good (and as I like to say, if the genes fit and feel good, wear them!) If you don't have a story like mine, use your imagination and make one up. Go wild! Wouldn't you feel different working on these pages if you knew that you had millionaire genes? Newsflash: Imagine with feeling that you do—and you DO! Take a moment now to clarify or dream up your own personal story of a wealthy ancestry. Ponder the power of carrying the combined hopes, dreams and talents of your ancestors in the very fabric of your soul. Capture the essence of your story on an index card and refer to it often. Your millionaire roots are just itching to bear fruit!

MILLIONAIRE'S TIP

Today would be a great day to set up a
Millionaire's Money Jar. This is where you
can "deposit" the coins, paper money
and other valuables you are likely to be
finding as this process unfolds. Keep your
Money Jar someplace handy and visible,
and fill it only with the money you find.
It will symbolize an open container, ready
to welcome and hold greater wealth.

Today's Date

/ /

18

DAY EIGHTEEN

Your total funds to
spend in full today is
$258,400

Today you receive $258,400 to spend. Jot down your items and their amounts.

No.	Items	Amount
	Total	**$258,400**

DAY
18

Insights from today's spending (optional):

_____

_____

_____

Ask, and it will be given to you; seek, and you will find; knock, and it will be opened to you. For everyone who asks receives, and he who seeks finds, and to him who knocks, the door will be opened.

Matthew 7:7-8

DAY 19

BE YOUR OWN COACH

Sometimes people setting out on a new venture like The Millionaire's MAP may get distracted, bogged down or even overwhelmed in the process. If you ever feel a little discouraged or confused, you may want to consider seeking out a coach. Yet did you know that you can also be your own coach?

Give this a try: Stop for a few moments and take an outsider's perspective on you. Imagine you are someone else, who's been observing your progress during the previous days and weeks. Write down at least three suggestions that you would share with you in response to the following questions:

- ❖ What better habits might you encourage?
- ❖ What changes of strategy might you suggest?
- ❖ What barriers get in your way, and how could you better address them?
- ❖ What advice would you give?
- ❖ How would you ensure that you made it through the process successfully?

Listen to the answers that come, and take some quick notes. You might put the top ideas on a few 3 x 5 index cards to keep yourself on track and seed some new habits. If it feels like you could benefit from another person's perspective, make a list of potential coaches and give the best one a try.

MILLIONAIRE'S TIP

What music inspires feelings of
abundance in you? Consider creating a
custom "Wealth Hits" CD or iPod® playlist.
This is a great way to keep the spirit of
abundance and prosperity vibrantly alive
in your daily life.

Today's Date

_____ / _____ / _____

SPENDING RECORD

19

DAY NINETEEN

Your total funds to
spend in full today is

$418,100

Today you receive $418,100 to spend. Jot down your items and their amounts.

No.	Items	Amount
	Total	**$418,100**

Insights from today's spending (optional):

_____

_____

_____

When a butterfly flutters its wings in one part of the
world, it can eventually cause a hurricane in another.

MIT Professor Edward Lorenz

DAY 20
THE BUTTERFLY EFFECT

In his research on weather prediction in the 1960s, Professor Edward Lorenz of MIT discovered something remarkable: even the smallest change at the beginning of his computer simulation experiments would radically affect all long-range predictions. What Lorenz discovered was this: something as small as the flapping of a butterfly's wings over a flower in Africa, creating a very minor disturbance in the atmosphere, could—theoretically and under the right circumstances—gradually build into a great wind that grows into a hurricane thousands of miles away over Florida. Lorenz called this phenomenon "sensitive dependence on initial conditions." Today it is known simply as the Butterfly Effect.

It may seem to you that this spending game you are playing in The Millionaire's MAP has little or no long-range effect on your life or the lives of others. Yet in reality, you are creating your own master butterfly effect. You do this by developing and strengthening a daily habit of thinking, feeling and living in greater wealth and abundance. This seemingly small daily exercise will build into a powerful force that lasts long after you finish it. In your mind and heart, you are now daily handling larger and larger sums of money—planning, spending, investing and enjoying! When your greater abundance begins to manifest, you will use the expanded wealth mindset you are practicing today to help guide your spending choices.

What really turbocharges the process? Fun! Have as much fun as possible in your imagination as you spend today's cash allotment. And remember the awesome power of your imagination that can, like the butterfly, lead to huge effects in your future. As the Sufis say: *The flapping of a butterfly's wings can touch a star.*

MILLIONAIRE'S TIP

Make it a point to initiate conversations
with wealthy themes. Ask people
what they would do with unlimited
abundance. Listen carefully to their ideas
and then contribute yours. As your daily
spending allotment grows, ask yourself
the same question. Words are power.
Use yours wisely.

Today's Date

___ / ___ / ___

SPENDING RECORD

20

DAY TWENTY

Your total funds to
spend in full today is
$676,500

Today you receive $676,500 to spend. Jot down your items and their amounts.

No.	Items	Amount
	Total	**$676,500**

DAY
20

Insights from today's spending (optional):

_____

_____

_____

99

The first peace, which is the most important, is that which comes within the souls of people when they realize their relationship, their oneness with the universe and all its powers, and when they realize that at the center of the universe dwells the Great Spirit, and that this center is really everywhere, it is within each of us.

Black Elk

DAY 21

THE REAL WORLD:
A MESSAGE FROM CRAZY HORSE

Black Elk once said of the great Native American Indian Warrior Crazy Horse:

Crazy Horse dreamed and went into the world where there is nothing but the spirits of all things. That is the real world behind this one, and everything we see here is something like a shadow from that world...

Over the last few weeks you have travelled regularly into that real world, the world of imagination, dreams and unlimited possibilities. You have planted powerful seeds of destiny. You have expanded the frontiers of your future to include more of your highest aspirations and desires. And hopefully you've had some fun with this process along the way. As you prepare to spend your final allotment today, remember this:

Your life is a testament to your strengths, wisdom and love (with thanks to my mom.)

I believe that every one of us has a higher destiny even if we aren't clear what it is. For me this exercise in abundance and unlimited thought has been a powerful life catalyst. Likewise, you have a golden opportunity and a sacred responsibility to discover and live your special gifts and genius. As Robert Kennedy once said, "If not us, who? If not now, when?"

My hope is that this process inspires you to live to your full potential and beyond— for yourself and for the world. In the weeks, months and years since I completed the test flight of The Millionaire's MAP my life has transformed, on many levels beyond the financial. I attribute much of that directly to the process you are about to complete.

Your real world awaits you.
Have fun spending your allotment of $1,094,600 today . . ..

MILLIONAIRE'S TIP

Today is a day to celebrate! It takes a lot of discipline to come this far. I suggest treating yourself to something special today, as a tribute to your "Inner Millionaire." Whether it's lunch or dinner at a nice restaurant with someone you love, a massage, or even a relaxed coffee in your favorite cafe, do something today to celebrate your commitment to living a full and abundant life.

Today's Date

___ / ___ / ___

SPENDING RECORD

21

DAY TWENTY-ONE

Your total funds to
spend in full today is

$1,094,600

DAY
21

Today you receive $1,094,600 to spend. Jot down your items and their amounts.

No.	Items	Amount
	Total	**$1,094,600**

Insights from today's spending (optional):

_____

_____

_____

One can never consent to creep when one feels
the impulse to soar.

Helen Keller

DAY 22 +
THE CATAPULT FACTOR

Congratulations! You did it.

I suggest allowing the process to settle into your consciousness over the coming days. Take some time to simply notice and enjoy your new and more abundant perspective. You may also want to occasionally refer to your Millionaire's MAP spending records and notes, if only for a few moments. My first experience with The Millionaire's MAP taught me to be expectant yet patient. During and after the process I started looking for and being open to greater abundance and new opportunities. Then they started to appear—sometimes in different ways or at different times than I had imagined, yet always in a delightful and exciting manner. It was like my wealth radar had been powerfully reactivated. I felt as if my abundance tractor beam had been switched on.

The Millionaire's MAP seemed to clear the way for the universe to send more great things my way. I also felt better able to capitalize on new opportunities as they arose, as I was now expecting them far more often than before. The process was and continues to be a great learning adventure. It's a clarification of values, purpose and priorities, and a journey to greater consciousness all wrapped together.

Sooner or later, you may wish to repeat The Millionaire's MAP. Perhaps at the same $100 starting level, or perhaps with additional zeros on the end of your starting amount (e.g., $1,000, $10,000). Just always make sure to begin Day 1 with a spending amount that starts with a 1 followed only by zeros. Then simply follow the Fibonacci Sequence: 1, 1, 2, 3, 5, 8, 13, 21… to chart your increasing daily spending path.

The key is to start with a spending figure that would feel natural if you actually went out and spent it on Day 1. When you start a new Millionaire's MAP it's best if you begin with a comfortable spending amount. That said, if your imagination is really fired up and you want to start a new Millionaire's MAP with $10,000, $100,000 or even a cool million, go for it! Personally, I have repeated the process a number of times. It works powerfully to energize and refocus you every time you do it.

I salute your desire and dedication to upgrade your life and live your greater purpose. It was an honor to share this process with you. May you experience a growing measure of wealth, health and fulfillment in every facet of your life after working with The Millionaire's MAP. I would very much like to hear your unique Millionaire's MAP story. You can contact me by email at MCross@LeadershipAlliance.com

Tenzin Gyatso, His Holiness The 14th Dalai Lama.

According to Buddhism, individuals are masters of their own destiny.
And all living beings are believed to possess... the potential or seed
of enlightenment, within them. So our future is in our own hands.
What greater free will do we need?

I feel that the essence of spiritual practice is your attitude toward others.
When you have a pure, sincere motivation, then you have right attitude
toward others based on kindness, compassion, love and respect. Practice
brings the clear realization of the oneness of all human beings and the
importance of others benefiting by your actions.·. When you engage in
fulfilling the needs of others, your own needs are fulfilled as a by-product.

My religion is very simple. My religion is kindness.

The Dalai Lama

FINALE
MY LUCKY SWEATER, NORAH JONES, AND THE DALAI LAMA

Who dares, wins.
British Special Forces Motto

In the fall of 2003 I launched a new Millionaire's MAP. On a bright Sunday morning in September, I sat down with a hot coffee in my favorite Starbucks near my home in Stamford, Connecticut and began the process. This also happened to be the same day the Dalai Lama was scheduled to speak at noon in New York's Central Park, about an hour's drive south. For several months, I had planned to drive into New York and hear him. Yet what unfolded over the course of that beautiful Indian Summer day I would never, in my wildest dreams, have thought possible. Was there a connection to my having started a new Millionaire's MAP that morning? Or was it all just divine coincidence? You'll have to decide for yourself. At the very least, the following story demonstrates that there is great power in being open and receptive to the unexpected...

As I sipped my coffee and daydreamed about how I would spend my cash allotment that day, I remember my spirits lifting with the familiar sense of magic and expectancy I always feel when doing The Millionaire's MAP. I carefully spent my allotment for that day on paper, mostly on my upcoming trip into the city. Then I drove into New York. As I arrived in Manhattan and approached Central Park on Fifth Avenue, the crowds grew larger and larger. The line to see the Dalai Lama was at least three people wide and must have stretched for a quarter-mile or more. Stuck in traffic, I pondered the sight. The line seemed to be moving like frozen molasses. Oh man! I didn't feel like waiting for hours and then, from the look of things, very likely missing the Dalai Lama's talk altogether. So, I drove the hour back home to Connecticut, with a sense of resigned disappointment. The day was not unfolding at all as I had planned. Oh well, at least it was sunny and warm. Maybe I'd go for an afternoon run when I got back...

As I neared home, I had an idea. Perhaps the Dalai Lama was appearing somewhere else in the New York area during this trip? When I arrived back at my house, I went onto the Web and searched. As it turned out, he was scheduled to briefly appear again in New York—at a special event in Lincoln Center that sounded very interesting. He was opening a concert to benefit the Tibetan aid organization called Healing the Divide. Now I was getting excited again. This sounded like a great opportunity to see the Dalai Lama in a far more intimate setting than in Central Park. There was only one catch: It was that same night. I called Lincoln Center—the event was completely sold out for months in advance. The ticket agent made attending seem all the more impossible when she said they would definitely not be releasing any tickets from anyone who failed to show.

I thought about the situation for a few minutes. There seemed to be absolutely no hope. The devil of doubt whispered in my ear: "Drive all the way back into the city? Are you nuts?!? You've already tried once to see him... Think of all the other things you could do tonight. Besides, they're sold out!" Then, it was the angel of opportunity's turn: "Hey, what do you have to lose? It'll be a great adventure! You can always find a way... Carpe momento—just go for it!" For a few seconds, I teetered on the fence of indecision; I could have gone either way. I came very close to just forgetting it all and going about the rest of my day. Then something inside shifted. I could feel myself rising to the challenge. I would find a way—or make one. Every wall is a door. Geronimo! Who dares, wins! "There must be a scalper there you could get a ticket from," I told myself. The scale tipped, back towards Manhattan.

So I prepared to make my second trip of the day into New York to see the Dalai Lama. For added good luck on this second attempt, I decided to wear the new blue sweater my sister Kerby had picked out for me when I had recently visited her and her young son (my nephew Matthew Joel) in Los Angeles. She told me it would bring me luck whenever I wore it. As I drove over the bridge back into Manhattan, the signs started appearing. One of my all-time favorite songs, very rarely played, came on the radio. As Art of Noise's *Moments in Love* carried me back to a great time in my life, I made a mental note of the present moment and where I was headed as I drove on. Soon I approached Lincoln Center, looking for a parking garage. On-street parking spaces in New York City on a Sunday evening are about as common as a UFO landing in Central Park. Then, magically, a car pulled out of a great space, right in front of me. A free parking space in downtown New York—very nice. It seemed to be another small sign. My sense of anticipation grew.

My "Lucky Sweater" sister Kerby.

I walked toward Lincoln Center. From a distance, I could see there were lots of people holding up signs out front. Great! Scalpers! I should easily be able to get a ticket now. So what if I paid a premium? It would be well worth it. Dalai Lama, here I come! As I got closer, I read the signs: "Will buy your extra tickets," and "Please sell your tickets; will pay top dollar!" Someone even asked me if I had an extra ticket to sell. This didn't look good. I pressed on and visited the box office. No luck; seemingly no way and no hope whatsoever to get in. Great. What do I do now?

I decided to make some time and check out the lobby. At least I could soak in the high energy and good vibes of the crowd. I used the restroom. I made a phone call. I noticed that there seemed to be an unusually high level of security for this concert. Of course—the Dalai Lama was here. I walked past one of the entrance points to the auditorium and hesitated for a few moments. I decided to start a conversation and connect with one of the ladies stationed there. What could I lose? I told her about my day, how I had come down to the city to see the Dalai Lama, turned around, then drove all the way back. We spoke for a few minutes as she admitted people into the concert. Shortly, I could hear the people inside clapping as the Dalai Lama came onstage. To make a long story short... she ended up doing something miraculous. "There must be an extra seat in there somewhere," she said, with a slightly conspiratorial wink. This was definitely a good sign. I was getting in! I profusely thanked this angel in disguise and went into the auditorium. Sure enough, there were a few empty seats in back. I sat down and marveled at my good fortune. If the people sitting next to me thought I was some sort of weirdo because of my continuous smile, so be it. My team of angels must be in commando mode tonight, I thought. How could they top this?

You could practically feel the electricity in the air. The Dalai Lama shared the heart of the message I was told he had shared earlier that day in Central Park: In essence, there is nothing special about him, as the sacred resides within every one of us. He also spoke of his happiness that technology was being used to support the Tibetan people and help preserve their culture. Although he was on for perhaps ten minutes, his energy and good will filled the air for the rest of the evening.

The concert was amazing. Tibetan monks chanted. Philip Glass, who had organized the event with Richard Gere, played the original theme music he had composed for the 2004 Summer Olympics in Athens. Tom Waites performed. Lovely Anoushka Shankar, Ravi Shankar's daughter, played the sitar. As she performed with her small band on stage, I remembered how I had missed seeing her play years before in California. I had even saved the flyer to remind myself to see her if I ever had the opportunity again. As the concert continued, I spied a free seat up in the front row and made my move. Who dares, wins, I reminded myself. When the concert was over, all the performers came on stage, along with Richard Gere, to a rousing standing ovation. What a great night this had been! By now I was getting quite hungry and began thinking of where I would eat when I left the auditorium.

As the people in the front rows waited for the crowd to file out I fell into a conversation with a nice English couple. Suddenly, someone near us said rather loudly, "Look—there's Elvis!" For a split second it sounded like a joke. We all looked around anyway... and saw singer Elvis Costello along the side wall.

I went over and shook Elvis' hand. As he greeted a few other people around me, I noticed a pretty woman standing behind him and in that same moment realized it was Susan Sarandon. Directly behind her stood Tim Robbins. Hmmmm... things were starting to get really interesting. I had always wanted to meet them both. I loved Susan in *Thelma & Louise*, and Tim masterfully played Andy Dufresne, the lead in my favorite film, Frank Darabont's *The Shawshank Redemption*. Tim and Susan were talking with a few other people, so I introduced myself to the man on my left and struck up a conversation. This fellow turned out to be a writer named Monk who was covering the event for a magazine.

Just then, a lady who seemed to be directing things arrived. She spoke quickly to Elvis, Tim and Susan, and then into her walkie talkie. "Do you want to go up and meet them?" she asked them. "Yes," they answered. "Alright, then we have to go now. Let's move." Who's "them"? I said to myself. The newly formed mini-entourage turned and fell into unified movement like a flock of geese in flight. We all headed for a side door, led by the lady with the walkie talkie. Monk and I, and a few others, followed in step. Something magical was in the air; at this point I decided to go with the flow. Our small group wound its way up some stairs, around corners and through more doors, until we came to the entrance of a small room. There were big burly guards at the entrance. As we approached the door I looked around at the group and felt my heart sink for a split second. Everyone seemed to be wearing special orange VIP tags around their necks—everyone except me! I quickly dropped that thought like a hot potato and continued my conversation with Monk. The guards waved us all through. Yet another sign. I was losing count.

I found myself in a small room with about 20 people. A tray came my way and I helped myself to an hors d'oeuvre. Tim and Susan did the same. I noticed there was not much in the way of food or drink in sight. Odd. I looked around as a few more people came in. It was a bit surreal. No TV cameras or hoards of reporters with flashbulbs going off. It was an intimate VIP gathering, evidently a low-key party honoring Richard Gere and Phillip Glass, and their efforts in producing the concert. Edward Norton was there. So was Tom Waites and his brother John, with whom I had a nice conversation. Richard Gere and his wife Carey walked in. She seemed very sweet. Anoushka Shankar was on the opposite side of the room from me, with a few others. As I observed some Tibetan monks talking in one corner, I thought the Dalai Lama himself might walk in at any moment. Then I remembered hearing how he went to bed very early in order to start his morning prayers at 3 am. I decided to mix and mingle.

Over the next hour or so, I ended up meeting and speaking with most everyone in the room. Tim and Susan were wonderful. Here I was speaking to Andy Dufresne! I joked with him, and asked if they were planning a sequel to *The Shawshank Redemption*. "Ah yes, the Zihuatanjo Blues," he said, smiling, referring to the idealic beach he and Morgan Freeman had ended the film on. I told him about my corporate consulting work and seminars, and how much it sometimes feels like acting. Before I could tell Tim how much his recent speech at the Washington Press Club had inspired me, a friend called him from across the room. We shook hands and I told him it was great meeting him. I made my way over to meet Richard Gere. Tired yet exuberant, he spoke of how the combined efforts of many talented people had made the evening possible. Richard was gracious and humble. I noticed that he made direct eye contact with me and everyone he talked to. He said he and Phillip Glass had been planning and working on the event for two years. Remarkable. He was very happy at how it had all turned out. I then spoke with Edward Norton and told him I really liked his work. I made my way over to meet Anoushka to tell her how much I had enjoyed her playing. Afterwards, I noticed the pretty girl next to her, who seemed a bit familiar. "That looks just like Norah Jones," I said to myself. Hey, wait a minute. It is Norah! Then I remembered... Norah was Anoushka's half-sister. I introduced myself to Norah, who initially thought I was a reporter. We talked for a few minutes. This evening was feeling more and more like a great waking dream.

My lucky-sweater sister Kerby had sent me a copy of Norah's enchanting CD *Come Away With Me* as a Christmas present the year before. This was months before Norah became an international sensation. After listening to it and contemplating her lovely voice and eyes, I remembered thinking it would be nice to meet her some day. A few months later she won an armful of Grammy's, her CD went to Number 1, and I'm sure millions of other people also wanted to meet her. The odds of meeting her in person had felt like the odds of meeting Ringo or Paul. I asked Norah how her second CD was coming, and if she felt any commercial pressure after the incredible success of her debut. She spoke of her commitment to her music, her artistic integrity, and about the challenges of new-found fame. She and Anoushka were lovely and refreshingly down-to-earth. It occurred to me that performing is just another job. These world-famous "stars," which so many people put on a pedestal, are just talented people doing their job. Performing is simply a way of expressing their creative gifts, gifts that inspire and delight so many. Many of the unique celebrities at this party also used their popularity to make a difference in the world. I sensed zero "celebrity ego" in the room.

I asked Norah and Anoushka if I could get a picture of us together. They agreed. My camera jammed for a moment; then the flash finally went off. I hoped we all had our eyes open. As the party wound down, a woman rushed into the room, a slightly worried look written on her face. I asked if anything was wrong. She said she was responsible for the party's drinks and food that night, which had never showed up. She immediately asked for everyone's attention, and said: "If anyone here would like to have dinner on the house, please raise your hand…"

Feeling quite hungry by now, I felt my hand go up with a mind of its own. So did Monk's, along with a few other people. The woman, whose name was Paula, rounded us up and made the arrangements. Another angel in disguise. We made our way to the lobby where a large cocktail reception was winding down. I stopped for a quick glass of champagne as our group assembled in the lobby for a cab. I noticed Daniel Goleman, author of *Emotional Intelligence*, nearby; I went over to introduce myself, and spent a few minutes talking with him and his son. We exchanged contact information. *Emotional Intelligence* is an excellent book, which I often use in my corporate presentations. *Very cool.*

Our dinner group took a cab to a lovely restaurant, The Blue Ribbon Bakery & Cafe, not far from Lincoln Center. As we walked to the front door, I saw a shiny penny on the sidewalk. Yet another sign. I picked it up with a smile. I must remember to go shopping for clothes with Kerby more often! Paula arrived and made sure we were seated and taken care of. Since we were all hungry, everyone ordered immediately. Dinner was absolutely delicious and filled with great conversation. When I shared the essence of my adventures that evening, Monk jokingly said we'd have to hang out together more often. When dinner was over, we thanked the restaurant staff, had our picture taken and all piled into a cab. When we arrived at my car, the final blessing of the evening occurred: My dinner party comrades graciously insisted on covering my cab fare.

The evening had unfolded like a magic carpet, beginning with my decision to head back into the city that afternoon. It was like I was being completely taken care of and looked after. Somehow, I never once reached for my wallet during the entire night. I walked into my house at about 3 am, still smiling to myself and shaking my head. The night had been an enchanted dream. It all seemed wonderfully impossible. How would anyone believe it? As I fell asleep, I wondered: Was it in any way connected to the way I had started my day? Would it have unfolded as it did if I hadn't begun a new Millionaire's MAP that morning over coffee?

The next day, I put the penny I had found the night before in my Millionaire's Money Jar. Then I headed out to have the pictures developed. Afterwards I made for the café and began filling in Day 2 of my new Millionaire's MAP…

Anoushka Shankar, Norah Jones and the author.

Wherever your heart is, that is where you'll find your treasure.
Paulo Coelho, The Alchemist

Make your own trail.
Katherine Hepburn

ACKNOWLEDGEMENTS

I considered a short and simple "there's too many great people to thank" acknowledgement paragraph. I decided instead to just go for it and list everyone I could think of who contributed in some way to this book. To all those who have offered their million-dollar support, wisdom and inspiration including especially:

My mother *Jan*, for your insight, love and support and for introducing me to the Golden Mean and the infinite canon of wisdom

My father *Matt*, for your special genius

My beautiful sisters *Janny* and *Kerby*, for making me smile

Jerry and *Esther Hicks* and *Abraham*, for your continuous inspiration, humor and timeless wisdom, and for contributing greatly to the inspiration for this book. Thank you Esther for the wonderful Million Dollar Bill gift all those years ago—I carry it in my wallet to this day and smile whenever I pull it out

Dr. Robert Friedman, friend and brilliant co-author on *The Divine Code of Da Vinci, Fibonacci, Einstein & You* and the lovely muse in his life, *Arihanto*

Gurumarka Khalsa, for your friendship, alliance and insight

Diana, for your divine presence, inspiration and input—and more than words can say

Carlos & Gilda Guzman, Peter Donovan, Rob & Stacey Mandel, Alex, Ioana & Andreea Samoilescu, Barbara Gordon, Jardar & Michele Nygaard, Penelope Penland, Lyn Sommer, Colin & Synthia Andrews, Donna Cignatta-Gleason & Daniel Gleason, David Ison, John Bolduc - thank you

Jaye, Lily, William, Matthew, Tessa, Carlito, Sophie, Galen, Emily, Isabella, Sofia, Olive, Sydney, Charlie, Dominick, Henry, Teddy, Ian and all the golden children

Dr. W. Edwards Deming, mentor without equal, who taught me that "there is no substitute for knowledge"

Linda Deming Ratcliff and *Bill Ratcliff*, for making me feel like family and for your much appreciated insights and support

Billy Mills, Oglala Lakota Sioux Warrior and 1964 10k Olympic Champion. One of the wisest, funniest and nicest people I've ever met, along with his lovely wife *Patricia*. Thank you Billy for inspiring me every day

Clare Crawford-Mason and *Robert Mason*, for your genius, inspiration and graciousness

Marshall Thurber, former colleague and mentor, for your general brilliance and for introducing me in-depth to the work of Dr. Deming

Jefferson Vander Wolk, for your boundless energy, wisdom, good humor and generosity

Neil Ducoff and the entire Strategies.com team, for your great friendship, support and humor over the years

Charlotte Sliva, for your inspiring faith and confidence and the great Inn of the Governors team

Rich Gagliardi, for walking the talk and running the run, and the great Waterway Café team

Cheryl Johnson, for your balanced insights, great humor and friendship

Sam Gerberding, for your friendship, rock-solid character and great humor

Grace Baltusnik, *Kieth Cockrell*, *Helen Eggers*, and all the great people of Bank of America

Teresa Tanner, *Michelle Zwelling*, *Shawna Shannon*, *Jesse Miller* and all the great people of Fifth Third Bank

Missy Weld and The Speakers Network team

John Michell, mentor and brilliant author of *The New View Over Atlantis*

Dr. Ron Sandler, friend and genius author of *Consistent Winning*

Jeff Klepacki, 3-time Olympic rower, World Champion, friend, alliance and great inspiration, and his lovely wife *Melissa*

Danielle Donello-Papandrea, for your alliance and wisdom; and her super husband *Rocco*

Stephany Thompson, for your great alliance, vision, candor and good humor

Stephen McIntosh, friend, Integral theorist, author; and his lovely wife *Tehya*

Michael Castine, fellow Fibonacci enthusiast and good friend

Anthony Robbins, for your boundless energy, inspiration and profound insight

Mark Victor Hansen, one of the first motivational speakers I ever heard; Mark, your contagious "Attitude of Gratitude" has stayed with me for over two decades now!

Bruce Hrovat; my good friend and alliance of Citizen's Bank

Jack Canfield; your writings and work are a great lift and gift

Rob Brezsny, for the abundant, laser-guided, funny, touching and priceless insights you share in your work and weekly via www.FreeWillAstrology.com

Bjorn Borg, 5-time Wimbledon and 6-time French Open champion

Robert F. Kennedy, for his compassionate charisma, wisdom, vision and hope

The Beatles - John, Paul, George and *Ringo*, for their endlessly inspiring music and spirit

The Dalai Lama, Richard Gere, Philip Glass, Tim Robbins, Susan Sarandon, Norah Jones, Anoushka Shankar, Edward Norton, Monk and *Paula* for a magic evening in 2003

Donald Trump, for reminding me to THINK BIG and for making me smile

Steve Jobs and the brilliant Apple Inc. and Pixar teams—Macs Rule! To Infinity and Beyond!

David Neeleman, for founding and leading JetBlue and making flying FUN

Leonardo Fibonacci, for his immense and timeless contributions to the world

Thanks another million to:

Tom Reczek of *618design.com* for your incomparable graphic design genius, patience and good humor

Dr. Lou Savary, for your genius editing support and general brilliance

Heather Slater for your editing mastery and our spirited working dinners

In addition to the above, all unnamed though never forgotten friends, alliances and mentors, and all of the wonderful participants in my seminars and workshops over the years, from whom I have learned so much

And thank *you!* It's been great meeting you in these pages. I hope we have the opportunity to correspond and perhaps connect in person one day

Lastly, thanks a million salmon to:
My fuzzy feline friend and frequent writing companion *Mackerel*, for walking on my keyboard while purring—and then climbing into my lap, reminding me to take a break, stop and smell the roses (or catnip?) and scratch behind his ears

The Japanese character for prosperity.

The whole world is conspiring to shower you with blessings...
Rob Brezsny, www.FreeWillAstrology.com

GLOSSARY

Abundance, Abundant
ABUNDANCE is a great or plentiful amount; fullness to overflowing; affluence, wealth. *ABUNDANT* means in plentiful supply, ample; abounding with, rich. From Middle English/Old French/Latin word roots meaning "to overflow." < *Definitions from The American Heritage Dictionary, Second College Edition.*

Appreciation Theory
Whatever you Appreciate, Appreciates (grows).
Theory that whatever you regularly appreciate *(focus on with your heart and mind, value through your attention)* will appreciate *(grow, as when a bank's assets increase when they appreciate)* in your reality.

Butterfly Effect
Theory that tiny, often imperceptible causes or changes at the start of any process can produce dramatic, exponential impact/effects. Also called "sensitive dependence in initial conditions." From MIT Prof. Edward Lorenz's weather prediction research and experiments, which intimate that the flapping of a butterfly's wings in one part of the world can eventually become a hurricane in another.

Chaos Theory
Exploration and explanation of the "higher order" in seemingly chaotic patterns or occurrences, evident in nature and behavior that were previously thought to be irregular or random.

Check from the Universe
A process for attracting wealth and abundance involving daily reflection on a large "check" from the universe made payable to the holder, as described by actor Jim Carrey.

Divine Code
Integration of the underlying Universal/Divine Design Code, as manifested in all of its micro/macrocosmic and seen/unseen forms, expressed through the *Divine/Golden Ratio, Divine/Golden Proportion, Golden Mean, Golden Spiral, Golden Star,* and *infinite Fibonacci Sequence* (0, 1, 1, 2, 3, 5, 8, 13, 21...) and associated 1.618 ratios e.g., 89÷55=1.6181818...

Divine Proportion
The point that divides any quantity, shape, form, line, time period, etc., into two parts that have a ratio of 0.618:1 to each other. Also the proportion revealed between successive numbers in the *Fibonacci Sequence*.

Elliott Wave Principle

Graphic interpretation of natural cyclic patterns of social or crowd behavior, based on *Fibonacci* numbers and ratios; first described by R.N. Elliott in 1934; championed in modern times by investment genius Robert Prechter, author and founder of Elliott Wave International.

Exponential

Growth at an increasing rate, e.g., the 0, 1, 1, 2, 3, 5, 8, 13, 21... *Fibonacci Sequence* progression.

Fibonacci, Leonardo (c. 1170-1250)

The greatest mathematician of the Middle Ages from Pisa, Italy; lived during the time the Leaning Tower of Pisa was being built. He introduced the western world to the *Fibonacci Trinity* (Arabic/Hindu numbers, Zero, the decimal point) and the infinite *Fibonacci Sequence*, which illustrates *Nature's Golden Growth Code*. Fibonacci has been virtually forgotten in modern times.

Fibonacci Numbers

Any of the numbers from the infinite *Fibonacci Sequence*, e.g., 0, 1, 1, 2, 3, 5, 8, 13, 21, 34, 55, 89, 144, 233, 377, 610, 987, 1597...

Fibonacci Sequence   0, 1, 1, 2, 3, 5, 8, 13...

The infinite sequence of numbers created via each successive number being the sum of the previous two, starting with zero: 0, 1, 1, 2, 3, 5, 8, 13, 21, 34... As the numbers in the sequence get *bigger*, the ratio between them gets ever *closer* to the *Golden Ratio* of 1.6180399... Numbers from the sequence can be found everywhere throughout nature. They appear to be a key design component of the universe via the associated *Divine Code*.

Fibonacci Trinity

The three-way combination of the Arabic/Hindu numbers (1, 2, 3...), Zero, and the decimal point, all of which were introduced to the western world by Leonardo Fibonacci (c. 1170-1250), the greatest mathematician of the Middle Ages.

Fractal

Any part that reflects the shape of a whole, e.g., as a piece of broccoli looks just like the whole bunch from which it was taken. Fractal geometry is present everywhere at all scales throughout nature. Essentially the same principle as illustrated via a *Hologram*.

Fractal Cognition Theory

Theory of the brain's ability to recreate a whole concept or learning from any key part or piece of that same concept or learning, as any piece of a hologram reflects the whole from which it came.

God's Code
Another way of describing the *Divine Code.*

Golden Cut
The .382 or .618 "cut point" on any line, shape, form, etc. Can be simplified to 38/62 or even 40/60

Golden Mean - See Divine Proportion.

Golden Ratio
The ratio of any small part to a large part or visa-versa which equals 0.618:1 or 1.618:1 or between any number in the Fibonacci Sequence to either the one preceding or following it, which always equals or tends towards either 0.618:1 or 1.618. Can also be approximately expressed as 62:38.

Golden Rectangle
Any rectangle whose length-to-width ratio equals 1.618... (the *Golden Ratio.*), e.g. playing cards, 3X5 index cards and debit/credit cards.

Golden Spiral
An exponentially expanding spiral, as in a nautilus shell or galaxy spiral, where the radii of any diameter are in 0.618:1 (*Golden Ratio*) relationship to each other.

Golden Star
Any equal-armed five-pointed star or pentagram, which always reflects the *Golden Ratio* and Divine Proportion in its design.

Hologram
A 3-D picture or image created with lasers through a special photographic process in which the whole original image can still be clearly seen in any piece or part broken off of the whole. The holographic principle of the part containing the pattern of the whole has been postulated to describe everything from the structure of the brain to the design of the universe. See also *Fractal.*

Imagination
The power of the mind to form a mental image or concept of something; such power of the mind used creatively; the ability to confront and deal with reality by using the power of the mind; resourcefulness. < *Definitions from The American Heritage Dictionary, Second College Edition.*

Millionaire's MAP™
A process of expanded imagination for increasing wealth, abundance and quality in one's life. It consists of spending money daily on paper in increasing amounts, as aligned with the infinite *Fibonacci Sequence.*

Nature's Golden Growth Code
The code underlying growth and expansion throughout the universe, as illustrated by the *Divine Code*.

Paradigm
The mental map, model, filter, belief or *theory* through which we see and interpret the world. The sum total of our paradigms comprise our mind's operating or navigational system, e.g., one with a prosperous paradigm/mindset sees the world as an abundant place filled with many opportunities. See also *Theory*.

Prosper, Prosperity, Prosperous
To **PROSPER** is to be fortunate or successful; thrive; to cause to thrive. From Middle English/Old French/Latin word roots meaning "to render fortunate." **PROSPERITY** is the condition of being **PROSPEROUS**: Having success, flourishing; well-to-do, well-off; propitious, favorable. < *Definitions from The American Heritage Dictionary, Second College Edition.*

Sacred Cut or Ratio - See Divine Proportion.

Theory
The critical basis for understanding, categorizing and learning from experience. Our theory acts a *paradigm* or filter; as Einstein noted, "It is our theory that decides what we can observe [or *not* observe]." An unexamined or stagnant theory is like relying on an unexamined or old map for navigational guidance into new territory. Without theory there is no basis for prediction, hence no learning and no opportunity for growth or improvement. New theory leads to new actions and new results. Continuously upgraded theories are vital for intelligent life navigation. The Millionaire's MAP theory? Exercising one's imagination—with feeling—around greater wealth and abundance can both attract it and help lead us there.

TimeMAP
A process for visually mapping the significant events in one's past, present and desired future life. For gaining greater insight, perspective and for stimulating one's imagination.

Ubiquitous
Being or seeming to be everywhere at the same time; omnipresent [e.g., the ubiquitous *Divine Code* can be found throughout the universe, at every level of the micro and macro worlds.] < *Definitions from The American Heritage Dictionary, Second College Edition.*

Wealth Collage
A visual collage, often consisting of pictures, drawings, key words and affirmations, representing one's ideal desired future. A powerful tool for positive focus, visualization and imagination.

ADDITIONAL QUOTES

It is better to give *and* receive.
Bernard Gunther

True genius lies in finding what's always been there.
William Devane, actor

That which is, GROWS; that which is not, BECOMES.
Galen (129-199 A.D.)

Obstacles cannot crush me. Every obstacle yields to stern resolve.
He who is fixed to a star does not change his mind.
Leonardo Da Vinci, Notebooks

I am certain of nothing but the heart's affections, and the truth of imagination.
John Keats

Friends are kind to each other's hopes. They cherish each other's dreams.
Henry David Thoreau

Set your goals to paper and you are halfway there.
Don Ward

What do most millionaires tell me they learned in their salad years?
They learned to think differently from the crowd.
Dr. Thomas J. Stanley, The Millionaire Mind

The way to win is to realize you already have. You can never lose in noble
and daring attempts to transform your life.

Ninety percent of the results we get come from only 10% of the actions we choose.
Are you clear about and focused on those vital 10% actions in your life?
Matthew Cross

Every situation, every moment is of infinite worth; for it is the representative
of a whole eternity.
Johann Wolfgang von Goethe

The most beautiful thing we can experience is the mysterious.
It is the source of all true art and all science.
Albert Einstein

The way you activate the seeds of your creation is by making choices about the results you want to create. When you make a choice, you mobilize vast human resources which otherwise go untapped. If you limit your choices only to what seems possible or reasonable, you disconnect yourself from what you truly want and all that is left is a compromise.

Robert Fritz

A goal without a method to achieve it means nothing.

If you stay in this world, you will never learn another one.

You will only get what your systems will deliver.

Dr. W. Edwards Deming

Surround yourself with people who believe you can.

Dan Zadra

As a single footstep will not make a path on the earth, so a single thought will not make a pathway in the mind. To make a deep physical path, we walk again and again. To make a deep mental path, we must think over and over the kind of thoughts we wish to dominate our lives.

Henry David Thoreau

He who would have beautiful roses in his garden must have beautiful roses in his heart.

S. R. Hole

There is no substitute for Knowledge.

Dr. W. Edwards Deming

MILLIONAIRE'S MAP
BIBLIOGRAPHY

WEALTH, SUCCESS & CAREER BUILDING

Paradigms: The Business of Discovering the Future
> Barker, Joel A. - HarperBusiness; Reprint edition: May 1993

What Color Is Your Parachute?
> Boles, Richard Nelson - Ten Speed Press; October 2003

What Should I Do With My Life?
> Bronson, Po - Random House; December 2002

The Success Principles: How to Get from Where You Are to Where You Want to Be
> Canfield, Jack, with Janet Switzer - HarperCollins; 1st edition: 2005

Don't Worry, Make Money: Spiritual and Practical Ways to Create Abundance and More Fun in Your Life
> Carlson, Richard; Ph.D. - Hyperion Press; October 1997

The Richest Man in Babylon
> Clason, George S. - Signet; Reissue edition: February 2004

Major In Success: Make College Easier, Fire Up Your Dreams, and Get a Great Job
> Combs, Patrick and Canfield, Jack – Ten Speed Press; 2007

The 4-Hour Workweek: Escape 9-5, Live Anywhere, and Join the New Rich
> Ferriss, Timothy - Crown; 2007

Ask And It Is Given
> Hicks, Esther and Jerry - Hay House; October 2004

The Amazing Power of Deliberate Intent
> Hicks, Esther and Jerry - Hay House; December 2005

The Shell Game: Reflections on Rowing and the Pursuit of Excellence
> Kiesling, Stephen - Nordic Knight Press: 1994

Rich Dad, Poor Dad
> Kiyosaki, Robert - Warner Books; April 2000

Financial Freedom: The Alchemy of Choice
> Koteen, Judi Pope (ed) - Indelible Ink; 1990

The Diamond Cutter
> Roach, Michael - Doubleday; July 2003

Awaken the Giant Within
>Robbins, Anthony - Free Press; Reprint edition: November 1992

Busting Loose From the Money Game: Mind-Blowing Strategies for Changing the Rules of a Game You Can't Win
>Scheinfeld, Robert: - Wiley; 2006

I Could Do Anything If I Only Knew What It Was
>Sher, Barbara - DTP; August 1995

Live the Life You Love: In Ten Easy Step-By-Step Lessons
>Sher, Barbara - DTP; February 1997

Do What You Love, The Money Will Follow: Discovering Your Right Livelihood
>Sinetar, Marsha - DTP; Reissue edition: March 1989

The Millionaire Mind
>Stanley, Thomas J.; Ph.D. - Andrews McMeel Publishing; August 2001

Trump: How to Get Rich
>Trump, Donald J., and Meredith McIver - Random House; 1st edition: March 2004

Trump: The Art of the Deal
>Trump, Donald J., and Tony Schwartz - Warner Books; Reprint edition: January 1989

The Trick To Money Is Having Some!
>Wilde, Stuart - Hay House; Reprint edition: April 1995

RECOMMENDED MOVIES
(in no particular order)

• *Trading Places* • *The Shawshank Redemption* • *Blade Runner* • *Crash*
• *Running Brave (The Billy Mills Story)* • *Rudy* • *The Matrix* • *V for Vendetta*
• *F/X* • *Bobby* • *The Secret* • *Rocky* • *The Truman Show* • *Aladdin* • *The Illusionist*
• *A Bugs Life* • *The Sting* • *Yellow Submarine* • *Catch Me If You Can* • *Cool Blue*
• *Papillion* • *Cousins* • *Good Will Hunting* • *School Ties* • *The Black Stallion*
• *The Verdict* • *Being There* • *Encino Man* • *Where Eagles Dare* • *Forrest Gump*
• *Dark Passage* • *Apollo 13* • *Rainman* • *JFK* • *Thunderheart* • *The Karate Kid*
• *Dances With Wolves* • *Pirates of Silicon Valley* • *Back to the Future* • *Goldfinger*
• *The Secret of My Success* • *The Graduate* • *MacKenna's Gold* • *The Mummy*
• *A Beautiful Mind* • *Executive Action* • *The Secret Garden* • *Star Wars*
• *The Lord Of The Rings: Return of the King* • *Singing In The Rain* • *Hildago*
• *The Little Princess* • *Star Trek: Insurrection* • *The Sound of Music* • *The Rookie*
• *Raiders of the Lost Ark* • *Groundhog Day* • *Stripes* • *Ghostbusters*
• *The Wind in the Willows* • *Out On A Limb* • *The Bourne Identity*
• *As Good As It Gets* • *GATTACA* • *Bill* • *Frequency* • *About A Boy*
• *The Wizard of Oz* • *The Iron Giant*

IMAGINATION, INSPIRATION & LEARNING

The Isaiah Effect: Decoding the Lost Science of Prayer and Prophesy
Braden, Gregg - Three Rivers Press; July 2001

Pronoia is the Antidote for Paranoia: How the Whole World is Conspiring to Shower You With Blessings
Brezsny, Rob - Frog, Ltd. 2005

Chicken Soup For The Soul: Living Your Dreams
Canfield, Jack, and Mark Victor Hansen - Health Communications; 10th edition: August 2003

The Alchemist: A Fable About Following Your Dream
Coelho, Paulo - Harper San Francisco; Reprint edition: May 1995

Flow: The Psychology of Optimal Experience
Csikszentmihalyi, Mihaly - Perennial; Reproduction edition: March 1991

The Instant Tarot Reader: Book and Card Set
Farber, Monte; and Amy Zerner - St. Martin's Press; September 1997

Dumbing Us Down: The Hidden Curriculum of Compulsory Schooling
Gatto, John Taylor - New Society Pub; 10th edition: April 2002

Creative Visualization: Use the Power of Your Imagination to Create What You Want in Your Life
Gawain, Shakti - New World Library; October 2002

How to Think Like Leonardo da Vinci: Seven Steps to Genius Every Day
Gelb, Michael J. - Dell; February 2000

The Prophet
Gibran, Kahlil - Knopf; September 1923

The Tipping Point: How Little Things Make a Big Difference
Gladwell, Malcolm - Little Brown & Company; February 2000

Ecstasy is a New Frequency
Griscom, Chris - Fireside; November 1988

The Secret Universal Mind Meditation (audio; 61 minutes)
Howell, Kelly – BrainSync Publishing; 2006 (www.BrainSync.com)

Zen in the Martial Arts
Hyams, Joe - Bantam; June 1982

Bringers of the Dawn: Teachings from the Pleiadians
Marciniak, Barbara - Bear & Co; September 1992

The New View Over Atlantis
        Michell, John - HarperCollins (paper); Revised edition: December 1985

Lessons of a Lakota
        Mills, Billy; Nicholas Sparks (contributor) - Hay House; July 2005

Summerhill: A Radical Approach to Child Rearing
        Neill, Alexander S. (Neill is my #1 educational visionary) -
Hart Pub Co; April 1984

Superlearning 2000: New Triple Fast Ways You Can Learn, Earn, and Succeed in the 21st Century
        Ostrander, Sheila; Lynn Schroeder - Island Books;
Reissue edition: July 1997

The Magic of Thinking Big
        Schwartz, David - Fireside; Reprint edition: April 1987

The Power of Alpha-Thinking: Miracle of the Mind
        Stearn, Jess - New American Library; reissue edition: November 1989

Ramtha: An Introduction
        Weinberg, Steven Lee, Ph.D (editor) - Sovereignty; 1988

Mindmapping: Your Personal Guide to Exploring Creativity and Problem Solving
        Wycoff, Joyce - Berkley Pub Group; Reissue edition: June 1991

DIVINE CODE, FIBONACCI SEQUENCE, GOLDEN RATIO/SPIRAL/MEAN

The Divine Code of Da Vinci, Fibonacci, Einstein & YOU
Cross, Matthew & Robert Friedman, M.D. - Hoshin Media; 2009

The Da Vinci Code
Brown, Dan - Doubleday; March 2003

The Power of Limits: Proportional Harmonies in Nature, Art and Architecture
Doczi, György - Shambhala; Reissue edition: August 1981

Infinity Movements Video
Friedman, Robert, M.D. - To order call: 505.982.1682

Fascinating Fibonaccis: Mystery and Magic in Numbers
Garland, Trudi H. - Dale Seymour Publications; December 1987

Leonard of Pisa and the New Mathematics of the Middle Ages
Gies, Joseph and Frances - New Classics Library; January 2000

Five Equations that Changed the World: The Power and Poetry of Mathematics
Guillen, Dr. Michael - Hyperion; September 1996

Mathematics for the Millions: How to Master the Magic of Numbers
Hogben, Lancelot - W.W. Norton & Company;
Revised edition: September 1993

Sacred Geometry: Philosophy and Practice
Lawlor, Robert; Thames & Hudson; April 1989

The Golden Mean Book
McIntosh, Stephen I. - order at www.now-zen.com

The Wave Principle of Human Social Behavior and the New Science of Socionomics
Prechter, Robert R. - New Classics Library; Reissue edition: June 2002

Consistent Winning: A Remarkable New Training System that Lets you Peak on Demand
Sandler, Dr. Ronald D.; Dennis D. Lobstein (Contributor) -
Rodale Press; October 1992

A Beginners Guide to Constructing the Universe: Mathematical Archetypes of Nature, Art, and Science
Schneider, Michael S. - Perennial; November 1995

Zero: The Biography of a Dangerous Idea
Seife, Charles - Penguin USA (Paper); September 2000

CHAOS & COMPLEXITY

Complexification
Casti, John L. - Perennial; Reprint edition: April 1995

The Quark and the Jaguar: Adventures in the Simple and the Complex
Gell-Mann, Dr. Murray - W H Freeman & Co.; Reprint edition: October 1995

Chaos
Gleick, James - Random House UK Distribution; October 1997

The Essence of Chaos (The Jessie and John Danz Lecture Series)
Lorenz, Edward - University of Washington Press;
Reprint edition: April 1996

Complexity: The Emerging Science at the Edge of Order and Chaos
Waldrop, Mitchell M. - Simon & Schuster; 1st edition: January 1992

GREAT GENERAL INTEREST

The Web of Life: A New Scientific Understanding of Living Systems
Capra, Fritjof - Doubleday; September 1997

Nobody in Charge: Essays on the Future of Leadership
Cleveland, Harlan; Forward by Warren Bennis - Jossey-Bass; April 2002

*Order From Chaos: A Six-Step Plan for Organizing Yourself, Your Office,
and Your Life*
Davenport, Liz - Three Rivers Press; December 2001

The New Economics for Industry, Government, Education
Deming, Dr. W. Edwards - MIT Press; 2nd edition: August 2000

The Hidden Messages In Water
Emoto, Dr. Masaru – Beyond Words Publishing, 2004

Cosmography: A Posthumous Scenario for the Future of Humanity
Fuller, R. Buckminster - Hungry Minds, Inc; February 1992

Fingerprints of the Gods: The Evidence of Earth's Lost Civilization
Hancock, Graham - Three Rivers Press; Reissue edition: April 1996

Birth of the Chaordic Age
Hock, Dee; Founder and CEO Emeritus, VISA International -
Berrett-Koehler; January 2000

Synchronicity: The Inner Path of Leadership
        Jaworski, Joseph - Berrett-Koehler; January 1998

To Seek a Newer World
        Kennedy, Robert F. - Doubleday; March 1975

The Seven Mysteries of Life
        Murchie, Guy - Mariner Books; June 1999

Strong and Fearless: The Quest for Personal Power
        Nuernberger, Dr. Phil - YES International Publishers, 2003

From Being to Becoming: Time and Complexity in the Physical Sciences
        Prigogine, Ilya - W H Freeman & Co.; March 1981

The Fifth Discipline: The Art & Practice of the Learning Organization
        Senge, Peter M. - Currency; October 1990

Secrets of the Great Pyramid
        Tompkins, Peter - HarperCollins (paper); October 1978

Beautiful Evidence
        Tufte, Edward R. - Graphics Press; July 2006

Spiral Fitness DVD series
        David Carradine, Rob and Marissa Moses,
        available at www.danceandmartialfitness.com

WEBSITES

www.LeadershipAlliance.com
Home site of Matthew Cross' Deming-based consulting and coaching organization.

www.Millionaire'sMap.com
The interactive site for this book.

www.TheDivineCode.com
Matthew Cross' and Dr. Robert Friedman's site for their books about the greatest secret in the universe.

www.Abraham-Hicks.com
Inspiring, timeless teachings on powerfully creating and shaping our reality.

www.FreeWillAstrology.com
Great insight, laughter and wisdom from Rob Breszny.

www.FourHourWorkweek.com
Home site for bestselling author Tim Ferris' book and breakthrough lifstyle design wisdom.

WEBSITES (cont'd)

www.618design.com
Golden Ratio design excellence in all mediums, including web, print
and publishing.

www.OnTargetLiving.com
Fitness and nutritional genius Chris Johnson's home site for vastly enhancing
your health, energy and longevity.

www.GoldenNumber.net
The web's #1 resource for all things Golden Mean.

www.ManagementWisdom.com
Dr. W. Edwards Deming knowledge treasury and video library.

www.GoodThink.com
Home site of bestselling author, speaker and master inspiration agent Patrick Combs.

www.BreathIsLife.com
Home site of Kundalini Yoga Master Gurumarka.

www.Now-Zen.com
Home of the beautiful, Fibonacci ratio Zen Alarm Clocks.

www.ElliottWave.com
Fibonacci-based investment organization founded by Robert Prechter.

www.SacredSites.com
Martin Gray's stunning collection of ancient sacred site photographs.

www.StarThrower.com
Great educational videos including paradigm pioneer Joel Barker.

www.TheraSound.com
David Ison's organization; peerless relaxing and therapeutic music and training.

www.TheEnchantedWorld.com
Amy Zerner & Monte Farber's "Enchanted World." Divination, learning and fun.

www.OrderFromChaos.com
Liz Davenport's site for peak personal and professional organization.

www.HealingTheDivide.org
Site of the outstanding Tibetan aid and education organization based in New York.

www.EdwardTufte.com
Site of the "Da Vinci of Data," information and graphics design mastery.

www.BrainSync.com
Acclaimed audio programs for meditation, relaxation, mind expansion and life
enhancement.

www.KungFuMoses.com
Site of Sifu Rob Moses and the Spiral Fitness System.

PICTURE CREDITS

A heartfelt THANK YOU to every person and source who graciously allowed me to include their excellent pictures in this book. Please know that every effort has been made to assure that all credits are accurately attributed. If any omission or discrepancy is discovered, please notify the publisher. Thank you.

Safe Combination, Golden Key, Stacked Coins, Starfish & Sand Dollar, Cornucopia Harvest, Goat (Cornucopia Horns), DNA, Nautilus Shell, Parthenon, Great Pyramid, Sunflower, Ocean Wave, Water Drop, Stack of $1000 Bills, Trophy, Rocket, Car w/Ribbon, Bamboo, Young Woman Praying, Coins on Cash, Whistle & Basketball, Butterfly on Flower, Catapult, Fireworks, Japanese Symbol for Prosperity, Cash Spiral, Sunburst Shell: *iStockphoto.com*

Spiral Galaxy: *NASA*

Millionaire's MAP Fibonacci-based Spending Graph, Cornucopia w/ Cash & Coins, Cornucopia Coins, Fibonacci Trinity, TimeMAP, Triumph Man Shadow, *School Ties* Location Shots, Vintage Couple, Anoushka/Norah & Matthew, Kerby, Gold Coin, Boston Public Library, Divine Code glyphs, Billy Mills and the Author: *Matthew Cross/author's collection*

Author's picture: *Diana Doroftei*

Millionaire's Check: *Tom Reczek*

Cornucopia on Currency: *FRBSF.org*

Vitruvian Man by Da Vinci, Albert Einstein by Yousuf Karsh, The Dalai Lama, Matt Damon: *wikipedia.org*

Leonardo Fibonacci: *Robert Prechter, Sr.*/The Elliott Wave Principle, by *Robert Prechter, Jr.*; *courtesy of the author*

Deming Prize Medal: *courtesy of JUSE/Japanese Union of Scientists & Engineers, Tokyo, Japan*

Billy Mills winning the 1964 Olympic 10k: *courtesy of Billy and Pat Mills*

Man/Gears/Earth/Universe (Flat Earth woodcut): *Camille Flammarion, 1888, from his L'atmosphère: Météorologie Populaire.*

God has put a secret art into the forces of nature and the human heart, empowering it to fashion itself out of chaos into a divine world filled with light, wisdom, love, abundance and laughter.

Immanuel Kant,
adapted by Matthew Cross

ABOUT THE AUTHOR

Matthew Cross is President of Leadership Alliance, a cutting-edge organization that provides breakthrough strategies for growth and transformation. He is passionate about helping people and organizations discover how to tap and optimize their genius, assets and opportunities.

A professional speaker, Deming scholar, success catalyst and Hoshin Kanri Strategic Alignment Specialist, Mr. Cross consults to Fortune 100 companies and lectures internationally. An avid runner, tennis player and ancient history researcher, he is also the author of the following books, published by Hoshin Media:

- *The Hoshin Success Compass*

- *The Golden Ratio Lifestyle Diet*
- *The Divine Code of Da Vinci, Fibonacci, Einstein & YOU*
- *The Genius Activation Quote Book*
  (all co-authored with Robert Friedman, M.D.)

- *The Little Book of Romanian Wisdom*
  (co-authored with Diana Doroftei)

- *Be Your Own President: A Handbook for Enhanced Personal & Professional Leadership (2012)*

Matthew Cross can be reached at:
Leadership Alliance
P.O. Box 16791
Stamford, Connecticut 06905

MCross@LeadersAll.com
www.LeadershipAlliance.com

In the long run, we only hit what we aim at.
Henry David Thoreau

NOTES

NOTES

NOTES

NOTES

NOTES

NOTES

NOTES

HOSHIN MEDIA PRODUCTS

The Golden Ratio Lifestyle Diet

The Golden Ratio Lifestyle Diet ventures boldly into new territory in health, nutrition and longevity—where no doctor, nutritionist or personal trainer has gone before.

by Robert Friedman, M.D. & Matthew Cross

Hoshin Media, 2011; 382 pages; illustrated. • $19.95

www.GoldenRatioLifestyle.com

The Hoshin Success Compass™

Map Your Way to Success with the Secret Alignment Process of the World's Greatest Companies.

By Matthew Cross

Hoshin Media, 2012; 100 pages, illustrated workbook. • $24.95

www.HoshinSuccessCompass.com

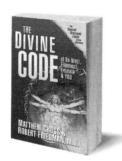

The Divine Code of Da Vinci, Fibonacci, Einstein and YOU

A treasure chest encyclopedia of the history, pioneering geniuses and practical applications of PHI/the Golden Ratio 1.618:1, the Secret Success Code of the Universe.

By Matthew Cross & Robert Friedman, M.D.

Hoshin Media, 2009; 660 pages; illustrated. • $29.95

www.TheDivineCode.com

The Genius Activation Quote Book

Activate your Innate Genius with these Classic Divine Code/Golden Ratio Quotes.

By Matthew Cross & Robert Friedman, M.D.

Hoshin Media, 2011; illustrated. 13.95

www.TheDivineCode.com

The Little Book of Romanian Wisdom

Discover the Unique Wisdom of Romania.

By Diana Doroftei & Matthew Cross

Hoshin Media, 2011; illustrated. • 12.95

www.RomanianWisdom.com

Made in the USA
Lexington, KY
30 March 2012